AMONG

AND FRA

BUILDING AN HON̲ᴇ̲ᴊ̲ᴛ BUSINESS

IN A HIGH-RISK MARKET

AMONG FRIENDS AND FRAUDSTERS

BUILDING AN HONEST BUSINESS IN A HIGH-RISK MARKET

MARIE ENGLESSON

NEW DEGREE PRESS

AMONG FRIENDS AND FRAUDSTERS
BUILDING AN HONEST BUSINESS IN A HIGH-RISK MARKET

ISBN   978-1-63676-604-1 *Paperback*
        978-1-63676-264-7 *Kindle Ebook*
        978-1-63676-265-4 *Ebook*

"You gotta do it with class and integrity. If not, you're gonna drag yourself through the mud."

— SOLOMON BURKE

TABLE OF CONTENTS

To Oliver, I'm sorry I didn't write you a "Paw Patrol" book. Perhaps you will like this book when you get older?

INTRODUCTION

———

I drove my car slowly down the backstreets of Msasani, an affluent neighborhood in Dar es Salaam, Tanzania. As usual, it was a hot and sunny morning. The temperature was already above thirty degrees Celsius. The sleepy dirt roads took me along the beaches of the Indian Ocean to the suburb of Mikocheni, where my office was. I listened to some songs on Spotify. I drove carefully to avoid the frequent potholes. I enjoyed the drive, the music, and the view, all of which gave me a short relief from my thoughts.

My startup, Atsoko, a beauty retail business I founded in 2012 and had been building for a few years, was in acute need of financing, which stressed me out. Today was the first Saturday of the year and also my first day in office after a short Christmas break. As with every year, the first day of the year meant a stock take. I didn't look forward to it. I hadn't really been able to relax over the holiday, and I felt tired before the year had even started.

Midmorning, when I had finally settled at my desk, I got a call from my custom clearing agent. We'll call him Alex. I had texted him just before for an update about our shipment that had been stuck in customs over the holiday. The clearing delay had already cost us a lot of money in storage fees and loss of sale.

"So, the custom clearing system is still down," he said. I could hear he was on the move. Alex was always on the move. He was quite efficient and the best clearing agent my company's had so far. I sighed because I knew what would come. "They can release it manually for us, but then we need to pay a little bit, you know, just some soda money," he said.

I went quiet for a bit. "How long do you think it will take before they get the system up again and can clear it otherwise?" I asked with another sigh.

"I'm not sure. Tuesday, Wednesday maybe?" he said. "For f*ck's sake," I said. Alex always got a bit uncomfortable when I showed my anger. "Pole Sana, Madam," he said, which in this case meant: "I'm sorry." He nervously cleared his throat and waited for my response.

I tried to assess the situation.

Another three to four days in customs would cost us much more than the bribe to this custom official. Would the official try to punish us if we turned him down? How much could it cost us to say no if he decided to punish us? Would this small bribe really make any difference in the long term? Was it really so bad to pay? What was the difference between paying this guy a bribe, compared to paying fees to the storage company who was probably corrupt anyway? But again, I didn't want to get into a cycle of bribery in customs. I didn't want to pay bribes.

What should I do?

All I really wanted was to get my stock take done and get the shipment out. How tempting it was to just pay and fast track our shipment to get the problem out of my way. I had enough issues to deal with.

* * *

Over the last twenty years, viewpoints on roles and responsibilities of the private sector in feeding corruption have shifted greatly. Before, bribes paid abroad by Western corporates were not legal, but also not illegal, as there wasn't any jurisdiction covering the practice. In most Western countries, including my home country, Sweden, bribes paid in foreign countries were even tax deductible as a business expense as long as you could provide some supporting document. This practice only started to change after the Organisation for Economic Co-operation and Development (OECD) convention in 1997 finally outlawed it, defining bribes paid abroad as illegal, and as such also non-deductible expenses.[1] Needless to say, for decades, international companies could pay bribes in foreign countries without any risk of legal repercussions in their home countries. That seems impossible today.

The big shift happened after 9/11 and the Iraq War when the West saw corruption come back to bite the hand that was feeding it. After the death of Saddam Hussein, hundreds of millions of dollars in cash were found hidden away in one of Saddam Hussein's luxury estates. By following the trail of money, the investigators were led back to international companies that had participated in the Oil-for-Food Programme run by the UN. More than two

---

1   "OECD Convention on Combating Bribery of Foreign Public Officials in International Business Transactions," OECD, accessed September 28, 2020.

thousand international companies, including household names such as Chevron Corporation and Daimler AG, were found guilty of paying bribes to Saddam Hussein's regime in return for contracts under the Oil-for-Food Programme, either as suppliers or buyers. Their bribes then contributed to finance the loyalty of Saddam Hussein's military and security services, directly contributing to the deaths of civilians and soldiers. It was blood money.[2]

After the discovery of how bribes paid by Western companies had financed war and terror, the US finally started enforcing their Foreign Corrupt Practices Act (FCPA), and the UK implemented their UK Anti Bribery Act as a part of their anti-terrorism agenda. Most European countries have followed and implemented anti-terrorism and anti-money-laundering acts which indirectly cover corruption, as bribes are often a source of illicit funding. Together, these multi-jurisdiction legislations have long arms and can go after any company that has paid a bribe in any country and trades on their stock markets. The US has to date been the most active pursuer, especially as they can go after any company that trades in USD.[3]

European companies lead the top ten list of the biggest fines settled under the FCPA, and two of them are actually Swedish. The telecom supplier Ericsson and the telecom operator TeliaSonera both were fined one billion dollars for using bribes to win contracts in foreign markets.[4] To me, it was surprising to learn this, as Sweden normally

---

2   David Montero, *Kickback: Exposing the Global Corporate Bribery Network* (New York: Viking, 2018), chapter 3.

3   Ibid.

4   Harry Cassin, "Airbus shatters the FCPA top ten," *The FCPA Blog*, February 3, 2020.

scores well in the corruption perception index rankings from Transparency International. This shows that just because a country has a clean public sector at home doesn't mean its corporates are clean.

* * *

The legal environment against corporate fraud has also seen a big shift over the last two decades, becoming stricter. The Enron downfall in 2002 became a milestone in this development. The Enron executive team was convicted of fraud and conspiracy. According to the judge and the jurors, the executives should have seen and known what was going on in the company. Following the Enron scandal, corporate executives around the world started to review their internal controls. Moreover, The Sarbanes Oxley Act was implemented to whip companies, at least listed companies, to ensure better internal controls against fraud.

Tough legislation is good. However, both my experiences in Tanzania and the research I have done writing this book have given me a much more nuanced understanding of fraud and corruption. Fraud and bribery are not rogue acts committed by a few bad international companies or a few bad high-level government officials with a criminal mind.

The 2018 global economic crime survey from Pricewater-houseCoopers reported that about one third of the over seven thousand companies surveyed had either been asked to pay a bribe or lost business to a competitor that had paid a bribe.[5] The same report stated about half of all companies globally had experienced several incidents of

5   *Fraud: The overlooked competitor, Global Economic Crime and Fraud Survey, Tanzania, 2018,* (Dar es Salaam: PricewaterhouseCoopers, 2018).

fraud or corruption during the last twenty-four months. In Tanzania, more than half, 57 percent, of the companies had experienced several incidents of fraud or corruption, with theft, bribery, corruption, and general business misconduct being main offences. The frequency of crimes was higher in Tanzania than globally, but it was not so much worse than in the rest of the world. In the 2020 report, the figures look more or less the same.[6]

Why are fraud and corruption so common? Why do companies, employees, and individuals pay and receive bribes and engage in fraud?

What I saw and what I learned was that honest people, with the strongest ideals and morals, can become dishonest when big temptations are put in front of them. Any business environment that has a weak rule of law, lax controls, and a forgiving culture provides opportunities for fraud and corruption. It can be in Tanzania, on Wall Street, or in large corporate companies. I saw what finally motivates an individual to actually engage in corruption or fraud varies greatly. The motivation can be pure financial pressure, the excitement of doing something that is not allowed, or to protect someone they love, admire, fear, or revenge.

Whatever motivation sparks it, committing a small act of fraud can bring you down a slippery slope. What dishonesty can bring in terms of money, power, or an easier life is enjoyable. However, the individual or the company then finds itself tangled up. The tracks left by a bribe need

---

6   *Fighting fraud: A never-ending battle. Global Economic Crime and Fraud Survey 2020*, (PricewaterhouseCoopers, 2020).

to be covered up, leading to accounting fraud and poten-tially the need for slush funds, both of which may have to be covered up if discovered. Doing so may lead to another bribe or the involvement of more people, and so on it goes. If not discovered and stopped, a single corruptive act may spread corruption across a whole industry.

Charles Duelfer, who led the investigation of the companies that had bribed Saddam Hussein in Iraq, made an obser-vation about the individual decisions of the two thousand companies that sent money to Saddam Hussein's bank account: "They make their own little micro decisions, then you put them all together and you have a macro outcome."[7]

* * *

I had to make hundreds of micro decisions about both fraud and bribery during my six years in Tanzania, similar to the example in customs above. The most rational short-term decision for me would have been to pay that bribe. Only knowing the long-term effect of bribery on my company kept me from paying. Some days it took all the resilience, and sometimes all the courage, I had to say no.

For moral support, I started to speak with more senior members of the business community in Tanzania and Kenya about how to deal with fraud and corruption. I spoke with fellow entrepreneurs, corporate employees, business leaders, auditors, lawyers, and investors in the East African region. How could I stop both myself and my employees from engaging in fraud and corruption? With this book, I want to share a collection of those lessons and experiences.

7   Montero, *Kickback*, chap. 3.

With the understanding that we can all become corrupt if tempted enough, I will argue that business leaders, employees, and investors need to identify and assess the different types of temptations they may face in their company and how they should respond. Corruption and fraud are especially multi-faceted in high-risk environments with a weak rule of law.

To illustrate, during my time in Tanzania I received several offers from suppliers to participate in tax evasion and money laundering schemes. I got offers from government officials to circumvent tedious health and safety regulations. Moreover, government officials also regularly extorted me for bribes, and I was frequently conned by fraudulent employees, fraudulent customers, and bogus suppliers. In a high-risk environment with widespread corruption, it is hard to stay honest.

* * *

In 2015, Tanzania scored a thirty out of one hundred on the Transparency International Corruption Perceptions Index. Business executives and experts put Tanzania's public sector somewhere between corrupt and highly corrupt.[8] In the World Bank Doing Business report, which is an indicator for how business-friendly the regulatory environment is, Tanzania ranked 131 out of 189.[9] Despite this, I had decided to venture there and set up a business, as a first-time entrepreneur, in 2012.

---

8   "Corruption Perceptions Index, Tanzania, 2015, "Transparency International, accessed September 21, 2020.

9   *Doing Business 2015: Going Beyond Efficiency,* (Washington DC: The World Bank, 2014).

At first, I saw my venture more as an adventure and a learning experience, rather than my life's work. I had started my career working for a global telecom operator in several African countries and saw the rise of the African markets. I felt I wanted to be a part of that somehow, so my own venture would be my MBA. But as the first years as an entrepreneur passed quickly, I got more and more invested and convinced I was on to something.

In 2015, Dar es Salaam was ranked as the most promising new mega city in Africa.[10] Tanzania had sustained a GDP growth of above 7 percent for several years and had a young population of forty-five million inhabitants. Vast reserves of gas had just started to be explored. The real estate prices were skyrocketing. The government was maybe corrupt, but stable, which convinced investors to come. The future looked quite promising for Tanzania. Atsoko started gaining some momentum. After three years of building the company more or less on my own, I had three stores up and running. In 2015, I managed to close a financing deal that meant I could scale up with more stores, sign on new beauty brands, and hire a management team.

But the petty fraud and corruption I had already experienced during the first three years escalated exponentially, both in frequency and value, as I scaled up. I had to deal with it, or I would fail. Besides the losses associated with the economic crime, the time and energy I spent on these problems took my attention away from developing the business.

---

10   Sam Sturgis, "The Bright Future of Dar es Salaam, an Unlikely African Megacity, "*Bloomberg CityLab*, February 25, 2015.

During 2016 and 2017, I grew my company, Atsoko, from a small retail startup to a beauty chain with seven stores launching more than ten new beauty brands on the market. Our revenue grew 100 percent over those two years with a half-million-dollar turnover, ranking Atsoko as one of the top one-hundred mid-sized companies in Tanzania. My brand and company became a household name among middle-class women in Dar es Salaam. Behind the scenes of the successful brand, my personal triumph was my success in fighting back the fraud and corruption, supported by employees and advisors I had come to trust.

Towards the end of 2016 and during most of 2017, Atsoko had almost zero incidents of internal fraud, and government agencies stopped approaching us as frequently for bribes. We had succeeded in building a stronger moral culture within the company which we also communicated to external parties, and we had learned to preventively detect and deal with the risks of fraud and petty corruption before they became a problem.

But then, just as I had started to exhale, a new type of regulatory risk emerged. The new administration, led by President John Magufuli, who had taken office late in 2015, started to implement very aggressive methods for tax collection, especially from the private sector. The chase culminated in a $190 billion tax bill to Tanzania's largest mining company, Acacia, in July of 2017, and the imprisonment of its managers for, among other offences, tax evasion. Investors fled, and Acacia crashed on the London Stock Exchange where it was listed.[11]

Atsoko was also targeted. This battle was different than the normal fraud and petty corruption I had managed up until then. I took the tax authorities to court in 2016 with a tax appeal, and in early 2018, I decided to finally sell Atsoko and leave Tanzania. I was done.

* * *

Corruption ruins the lives and futures of individuals, businesses, and societies. I have seen it firsthand. The deception that goes into corruption and fraud damages the societal trust we need to function and work together. When government officials accept a bribe, they betray the very citizens they are employed to protect. When a company engages in corrupt practices, it deceives its investors, customers, and employees. When employees deceive their employer and their colleagues, they hurt their company from within. When a political leader abuses the law for his personal gain or his own political goals, his means no longer justify the ends. He goes against the principles of natural justice a society needs to function.

I can't express how much I admire the local entrepreneurs, business managers, and employees in Tanzania who continue to get out of bed every day and get to work, knowing that their hard work and endeavors

---

11   Zandi Shabalala et al., "Barrick's offer for Acacia Mining reflects Tanzania risk: CEO", *Reuters*, May 24, 2019.

could one day all be in vain and taken away from them by corruption.

It is for them, especially, I have written this book.

The private and the not-for-profit sector play a pivotal role in either feeding or resisting corrupt practices at home and abroad. All small and large local and foreign organizations alike play an important role. It is a heavy responsibility especially for managers to carry, and I know that. It can be extremely hard to stay true and honest at times, and it takes resilience and courage.

This book is a guide for investors, donors, entrepreneurs, managers, and employees in the private as well as the not-for-profit sector. With this book, I hope to inspire people and organizations to stay true and honest, especially when it is hard. You can't enter a high-risk market with your eyes closed. Ignorance is not a valid excuse under the law and you may lose money as well as your reputation. Protect yourself and your company by understanding how fraud and corruption work before you get trapped.

* * *

The first part of this book will give different tools for understanding the psychology of fraud and corruption. Theories of behavioral economics will help you understand what corrupts us and why certain temptations are so hard for us to resist. You will find the stories of the ambitious corporate employee who was blacklisted by the World Bank for bribery, the wife who defrauded her husband, and the switch engineer who tricked major telecom suppliers in an elegant fraud scheme.

The second part consists of the insider's guide on how to build an honest company that can stand resilient against the temptations of dishonesty from within. A company which manages its internal risks will also get better at managing its external risks. I will tell the story of the corporate manager who refused to pay a bribe and waited two years for a permit, just to communicate his zero tolerance to corruption. I will share the story of how I finally found and built my own great and honest team. I will thereafter show how a company can map, assess, and manage external risks and give concrete advice on how to manage fraudulent customers and suppliers and how to manage cases of coercion and extortion for bribes.

As much as I think we need to talk about corruption, I recognize that talking about corruption does indeed pose some legal and reputational risks. Therefore, I have decided to make some of my sources anonymous and leave out some details.

PART I

HOW DO WE BECOME CORRUPT?

CHAPTER 1

WHY I WROTE THIS BOOK

———

By sharing my own successes and shortcomings in managing common petty fraud and corruption in Tanzania, I want to show how much these business risks matter to smaller businesses and why a successful manager has to deal with them in order to keep from going under.

THE JANUARY SYNDROME

In the afternoon on the same Saturday I had dealt with the situation in customs described in the introduction, I got a call from the sales attendant at our store in Quality Centre, a shopping mall near the airport in Dar es Salaam. Some officers from the fire inspection department were there, checking if all businesses had their "Fire Inspection Certificates." If a company lacked a certificate, there would be a fine to pay. My sales attendant couldn't find the certificate and was anxious. Thankfully, I could direct her to the certificate so she could locate it. We were reprimanded by the officials for not having posted their certificate on our wall together with all other certificates from various government agencies. We expressed how sorry we were, but we explained we had not yet had the time due to the recent holiday.

As I hung up after that call, I suddenly remembered that this was the week of the "January Syndrome." Petty corruption has a seasonality due to many of the lower level government officials living from hand to mouth. Largely dependent on bribes to pay school fees and to take care of an extended family, their solicitations for bribes would increase at the end of each month just before payday, at the end of year before Christmas, and then especially early January—hence the term January Syndrome. In January, lower level government officials were in extra need of some cash as they had school fees and rents to pay and had empty pockets after the holidays. I often felt for them, but they made my life very hard.

* * *

Government officials continued to approach us during the following week. When researching for this book, I found some notes in my diary from that week which helped me to remember some illustrative examples.

On Monday afternoon of that week, I was sitting in my office finishing up the stock reconciliation with my accountant when four immigration officers drove into our office compound in a big white Toyota Land Cruiser with tinted windows.

The immigration officers had become regulars at our shops and head office after they had arrested one of my interns for not having proper documentation. More about that story will be shared later in chapter nine.

As they showed up, I got a bit nervous. My investor permit had been approved, but it was not yet issued, despite the help of an expensive and prestigious law firm I had hired. Theoretically, as long as the permit was only approved, but not yet issued, I should probably not be in the office even though I owned the business. So, the immigration officers could create trouble if they wanted to.

All four of the immigration officers lingered around my store, picked up some products from our shelves, and implied that I shouldn't be working if I couldn't show them my permit.

"Well, then I will need to close the business and my staff won't get paid," I said, looking at the three employees who were also in the shop. As I felt my employees' silent support, I became a bit braver. "I won't give you anything, so please stop coming here to harass us." My pulse was racing, and I was biting my cheeks; but I tried to look calm and casual as I said it.

The female immigration officer went wide-eyed and said she felt offended. "We are just here to make sure there are no illegal workers here," she said. "I understand," I said, softening my tone a bit. The four officers left after a while, and the lady even purchased some products.

I felt proud I stood up to them this time. The assurances from my law firm of my permit being approved had given me the courage to do so, but I was still afraid because

I knew my bold move could have repercussions if I had offended them.

On Tuesday of the same week, one of my employees, we can call him Rashid, was stopped by the traffic police when transferring some new display stands from our warehouse to one of our stores. I had signed and stamped the usual letter confirming that Rashid was an employee with Atsoko and allowed to transfer the goods.

The police had stopped Rashid many times before, so we knew the drill. But this time, the traffic police went to the extreme and wanted to see import documentation of the goods and copies of various company certificates. The regulation allowing them to hold Rashid like this was unclear, but they wouldn't let him go. Rashid finally paid them some "soda money," after he had argued with them for thirty minutes.

WHY PETTY CORRUPTION MATTERS

Corruption is defined as "the abuse of entrusted power for private gain" and includes a wide range of activities.[12] Bribery is the most well-known type, but any type of power abuse can be considered corruption. Nepotism, for instance, refers to the hiring or promotion of a family member or a friend to a role they are not qualified for.[13] Petty corruption, the type of corruption I experienced the most as a small business owner in Tanzania is defined as "everyday abuse of entrusted power by public officials in their interactions with ordinary citizens, who often

---

12   "What is corruption?" Transparency International, accessed October 10, 2020.

13   "Nepotism," Transparency International, accessed October 10, 2020

are trying to access basic goods or services in places like hospitals, schools, police departments and other agencies."[14] Petty corruption is commonly linked to the use of coercion or threat in combination with the demand of a bribe. This practice is also called extortion.[15]

As a retail and distribution business, Atsoko required hundreds of permits to operate legally in Tanzania. The application process for permits often required between ten and twenty supporting documents each, all printed, signed, stamped, and sometimes certified by a law firm or similar. A corrupt government official could easily stall an application by losing a document in our file, or even the whole file, so that we would have to restart our application. The corrupt official would look for any minor reason to reject an application, such as missing stamp or a signature he or she felt was not consistent.

The officials were, of course, not available by e-mail or phone, so we would have to go to their office and meet them in person to follow up on our file. This could mean one to three hours in traffic and two to three hours of waiting time at the office—a whole working day lost.

I spent a couple of months of my life waiting in government offices like that—sitting and waiting restlessly in offices painted a flaky pastel green or yellow and badly lit with a few randomly placed fluorescent lamps. I used to look at the other people waiting with me. They were employees working at larger companies or small business owners, all waiting to see a government official.

---

14   "Petty Corruption," Transparency International, accessed June 15, 2020.

15   "Extortion," Transparency International, accessed October 10, 2020.

Some of them were sleeping, most of them were on Facebook or YouTube, and some of them watched the local soap opera showing on the TV that was always on in some corner. The air conditioning seldom worked.

Eventually, I got fed up with waiting, and as I didn't want to pay bribes to fast track, I took the time to learn how to deal with this petty corruption. Moreover, I realized managing petty corruption well would become a competitive advantage for us when partnering with foreign businesses wanting to enter Tanzania. Many of our suppliers, the American company Revlon, for instance, were liable for bribery in foreign markets under the US Foreign Corrupt Practices Act (FCPA). They were bound to assure their distributors in foreign countries also don't engage in corruption on their behalf.[16] We had to be able to assure them we wouldn't pay bribes to get their products out of customs, or they might not dare to enter the market with us due to the reputational risk.

I understood the only way to beat the government officials in an honest way was to learn the law better than them so we wouldn't end up in an endless cycle of permit applications being submitted and rejected for minor reasons. Even if corruption is widely accepted, it is still illegal, and if we could threaten to escalate an unfair delay, legally if needed, the government official who tried to play us would normally get a bit cautious. The Tanzanian judiciary system was slow, but it was still there. How I

16 US Department of Justice and US Securities and Exchange Commission, *Resource Guide to the US Foreign Corrupt Practices Act,* (Washington DC: 2012).

beat petty corruption will be described in detail in the ninth chapter

WHY FRAUD MATTERS

Internal fraud was, besides petty corruption, one of the business risks which preoccupied me the most in Tanzania.

The common characteristic for all fraudulent and corrupt activities is the fact that they are acts committed by an individual or a company for their own personal gain. The key difference between fraud and corruption is that corruption is often committed through the use of a threat of force and the abuse of power, while fraud is done through the use of deceit.[17]

There are many different types of fraud that may impact a company. The 2018 biannual economic crime survey from PricewaterhouseCoopers (PwC) lists several different types of corporate fraud: accounting fraud, fraud committed by the consumer, human resources fraud, and procurement fraud.[18]

Internal staff was responsible for two-thirds of the corporate fraud impacting companies in Tanzania, according to the 2018 PwC survey. And about half of the internal fraudsters were junior staff.[19] This describes very well what I experienced in my own company, Atsoko.

17   *Encyclopaedia Britannica Online,* Academic ed. s.v., "Fraud," accessed October 10, 2020.

18   *Fraud: The overlooked competitor,* PricewaterhouseCoopers, 2018.

19   *Ibid.*

THE LAST STRAW

Over the first four years of operation, I had to fire about fifty staff members, mainly within the sales and marketing team, due to some type of fraudulent activity or poor work ethic.

To operate a retail chain with several branches in different locations requires discipline among the retail sales staff. Staff coming late, disappearing during the day, taking a nap behind the counter, doing some type of side hustle during working hours, or skimming customers by increasing prices all affected our sales. Motivating and retaining young staff who came from quite challenging environments was difficult. I was not an experienced manager of sales teams, so I struggled.

What finally pushed me to see internal fraud as a major challenge for the company was what happened in late 2015. I thought I had finally gotten a really good sales team of people who were bright, energetic, and motivated. It was fun to see them selling, and the atmosphere of the company was great. Or, at least that was what I thought.

* * *

That year, Atsoko launched a campaign to recruit more customers. We printed thousands of catalogues with a voucher giving all new customers 20 percent off of their first purchase, and we distributed the catalogue across shopping malls and offices in Dar es Salaam. It was the major marketing spend for the company that year, and we were excited to see its contribution to our sales.

Some weeks after the start of the campaign, my business controller, we can call her Anna, noticed some weird numbers in our store in Kariakoo, a busy trading district in Dar es Salaam.

"Marie, almost all clients are new clients this month," Anna said. She was hunching over her laptop looking intensely at her screen.

We were sitting at our desks next to each other in our small office, so I stood up and peeked over at the numbers on her computer. Outside the office window, the green palm trees were gently swaying in the softening afternoon sun. We looked at each other and went silent. I could feel my heart sink.

Our regular, loyal clients normally represented about thirty to forty percent of our sales, and now they were close to zero. It meant almost all sales in the Kariakoo store were coming from new clients and subject to a twenty percent discount, which seemed quite improbable.

"Oh no," I said and rubbed my forehead. We were getting close to Christmas, the busiest season of the year. We had invested so much in this campaign and in training of our sales staff to start the busy season well prepared. We couldn't afford to deal with fraud and to lose staff members now.

Anna had started with Atsoko as an international trainee earlier that year. She had grown up in Eastern Europe, post-communism, and she had—thanks to her background—developed a good nose for fraud and corruption. You wouldn't guess when you saw her rather timid posture, but she was tough and paranoid in a very resourceful way.

We put together a plan that afternoon. Because we didn't have any closed-circuit television (CCTV) installed in the store yet, we had to spy on our sales staff in person in Kariakoo. We explained our suspicions to the manager in charge of the store and asked her to go with some back-office staff and approach clients coming out of the store. They had to pretend to do a survey and ask if the client had been offered our new client discount.

The report management came back with was not encouraging. They had quickly met several clients who had not been offered a discount in the store. When we cross checked the sales tickets against our sales system, a discount had been applied. The sales staff had simply pocketed the discount after the client had left the store. We contacted some of the clients to get affidavits so we could present this to our sales staff as evidence. Several of the clients had already guessed we were checking on our staff and readily helped us out.

Two staff were clearly leading the scheme in the Kariakoo store, so we decided to swiftly terminate our contracts with them before they understood we had caught them. We didn't want to risk them running away with keys, money, or stock. The dismissals of the two sales attendants were therefore quick.

Sitting across from me at my desk in the office the next morning, the first sales attendant, in her early twenties and with a university degree, took the news without a frown or an apology. She knew exactly what she had been doing, and I suspected she was the brain behind the scheme. She had not gotten on well with the new store manager, which was a possible reason for scheming.

The second sales attendant was a young, vibrant, and talented salesperson. She could drag clients into the store and sell them whatever. I liked her a lot. She was perfect for the store in the busy Kariakoo district and was, by far, our best salesperson there.

She started crying as we presented evidence of corrupt sales done in her name and explained we needed to let her go.

"Please, can I get another chance?" she asked.

She didn't have any education beyond primary school, and I knew this was a big blow for her. It would be hard for her to find another good job. I wished I didn't have to fire her; it would be another loss to the company, and I really felt for her. But I just had to get on with it.

The reasons this fraud became such a game changer for the company were partly because the losses were much higher than in previous fraud incidents due to the collusion of several people on the sales team. But more importantly, I had, for the first time since I started the company, a management team around me who became as upset as me when their colleagues defrauded them and as motivated as me to root out the fraud. I was no longer on my own.

Anna became my prime fraud fighter. Together we mapped out the fraud risks in the sales processes and implemented better systems and processes. Finally, we fully implemented a good sales and inventory system that would allow us to check cash and stock in real time. We implemented CCTV in all sales locations to be able to look closer at certain transactions or stores when we got suspicious. And we made sure we enforced our zero-theft employee policy; anyone stealing would be fired.

Besides Anna, I had also recruited three store managers who all were recent graduates and had international sales exposure. They took charge of the sales team and became responsible for recruitment, training, and performance management. They did a much better job than what I had done.

The ugly thing with fraud, and especially internal fraud, is that it fuels distrust between employees and between employees and managers. Internal fraud makes it very hard to scale up a business like Atsoko. A company can implement certain controls, but in the end, all systems can be circumvented as the following chapters will show. And as PwC states: "The cost of economic crime is not limited to financial/monetary loss but includes the cost of investigation, operational time wasted, and the general impact on the organization's reputation."[20]

CONCLUSIONS

As the sole founder, and sole manager, of my startup for several years, I had to dedicate tremendous time and effort to manage petty fraud and corruption. It was painful. Every time I was impacted by an internal fraudster, it broke my heart. I had hired and trained the employee, worked alongside them, and then they turned their back on me.

20 *Fraud: The overlooked competitor,* PricewaterhouseCoopers, 2018.

While taking away a lot of the joy and excitement of building a company, the experiences also made me a better manager. With time, I started to understand what made some employees steal or what weaknesses a government official had exploited to request a bribe. Eventually I understood that, as a manager, I played a big role in supporting my team not to surrender to fraud and corruption.

In the next chapter, I will dive deeper into understanding what motivates people to engage in fraud and corruption. To me, this knowledge became cathartic. I will also share some of the lessons I learned from senior members of the business community.

CHAPTER 2

IT'S NOT ALWAYS ABOUT THE MONEY

———

"It's easy to be judgmental about crime when you live in a world wealthy enough to be removed from it. But the hood taught me that everyone has different notions of right and wrong, different definitions of what constitutes crime, and what level of crime they're willing to participate in."[21]

- TREVOR NOAH

Why does an honest person become corrupt? And why do some people stay honest, while others falter? I wanted to explore the "why" of what corrupts us.

Internal fraud was, as mentioned, one of my major management challenges as a small business owner in Tanzania. And I'm not alone. The PwC surveys show, year after year, more than half of all economic crimes globally that

---

21   Trevor Noah, *Born a Crime: Stories from a South African Childhood* (London: One World, 2016), page 212, Kindle.

impact companies are committed by their own employees or their own staff often in collaboration with external parties.[22]

I find internal fraud fascinating as it is, in a way, one of the most corrupt acts a person can commit. The fraudsters are deceiving their own employer, their friends and colleagues, their business partners, or even their own family for their personal gain. Moreover, it is often a previously honest employee who commits the internal fraud. I tried to understand the forces at play which make an honest person corrupt.

CORRUPTION FOR SURVIVAL

In one of my interviews for this book, I spoke with Alfonso Rodriguez, a friend and a former top corporate manager for an international cement manufacturer. He has spent most of his career in emerging markets in Africa, and I have heard many stories from his work over dinners and drinks.

I asked him if he could describe the type of fraud he has encountered most frequently during his career.

He went quiet for a bit, then he said: "I would call it corruption for survival. Often people don't steal to get rich but to survive. Regardless if it is at low level or at high level, people steal for survival, or think they steal for survival."

He told me about a small town in a sub-Saharan African country where he spent some time a decade ago.

---

22   *Fighting fraud: A never-ending battle,* PricewaterhouseCoopers, 2020.

"The whole town and surrounding villages were dependent on a cement plant that had been set up in the 1960s; it employed more than 1800 people."

Alfonso was there for an extended due diligence as his former employer was about to acquire the plant.

Alfonso told me he was sitting idle waiting for a meeting when he saw the medical clinic of the plant. The medical clinic was the only one for miles, and all the people from the town and surrounding villages came there.

"I had some time, so I got curious about the clinic and the work they did. I walked over there and asked the staff about the most common things that workers sought medical aid for. They told me it was leg burns on the side of the legs. I found it a bit odd and asked to go through their logbook. About ten-to-fifteen people per day were treated for this, and the burns were most common among the staff in the maintenance and dispatching teams."

Alfonso was impressed with the clinic and especially by the doctor, who had on his own initiative set up an improvised post-natal care unit, using chicken heater lamps to keep prematurely born babies warm.

"But, I couldn't let go about those leg burns, so I went back to the clinic after my meeting to understand why the leg burns were so common. Workplace safety was an important part of the due diligence," Alfonso said.

After some investigations, the answer became clear. The maintenance and dispatching teams responsible for packaging and cleaning up the cement had sewn extra deep pockets in their pants, so they could put two-to-three kilograms of stolen cement in each leg. In the heat and humidity, their sweat created a chemical reaction with the cement burning their legs.

In total, sixty-to-seventy staff members were participating in the fraud scheme.

"What did you do then?" I asked Alfonso.

"Well, our job was to stop them from continuing this practice, so for some time we forbade them to wear pockets on the pants," Alfonso said. "But the workers also got pay increases, and eventually they got their pockets back."

The doctor of the clinic was of course in on the scheme.

"None of these cement workers were stealing to become rich; they stole out of survival," said Alfonso. "When we took over the plant the people were making about sixty-to-seventy dollars per month. The fifty kilograms of cement they could steal each month, they could sell for perhaps twenty-five dollars. And the doctor probably used any extra money he got for the clinic and those chicken lamps," Alfonso continued.

The cement workers made two dollars per day, which is just at the upper level of what the World Bank defines as extreme poverty.[23] It is easy to understand why the cement workers stole cement. The more interesting question, is why didn't all the workers in the cement plant steal when they must all have been under financial pressure? Only 4 percent of the workers were involved in the deep pocket scheme. There seems to be something else

23   "Poverty," The World Bank, accessed October 10, 2020

than financial pressure needed for a person to commit internal fraud.

THE FRAUD TRIANGLE - AN INTRODUCTION

In his book *The (Honest) Truth About Dishonesty: How We Lie to Everyone—Especially Ourselves*, behavioral economist Dan Ariely states most of us will cheat and lie at some point in our life. He further argues humans are, by nature, attracted to what dishonesty can offer. What then saves us from the temptation is our equally strong desire to think about ourselves as honest and good people and to be seen as honest and good people by others. Those are the ideals we have normally been raised and brought up with. In order to do something dishonest and still keep our image of ourselves as good people, we lie to ourselves and tell ourselves what we are doing isn't really our fault or so bad.[24]

I find Ariely's explanation of dishonesty scary, comforting, and quite correct. Comforting because he explains dishonesty as something fairly natural and not necessarily evil. Scary because his definition means everyone around me could try and deceive me. Correct because I can admit to doing it myself, and I have seen a lot of otherwise honest people excuse corrupt behavior both to themselves and others. I will expand more on Ariely's theories in the following chapters.

To understand more about internal fraud specifically, I decided to interview Kang'e Saiti, a Kenyan professional

---

24 Dan Ariely, *The (Honest) Truth About Dishonesty: How We Lie to Everyone – Especially Ourselves* (New York: HarperCollins, 2012), Introduction. Kindle

who is head of assurance at PwC East Africa. I wanted to hear his view on why some people engage in fraud and why others manage to resist. Saiti has spent most of his twenty-three-year career conducting internal audits and audits for companies and organizations in East Africa. He is well acquainted with behavioral forensics.

"The fraud triangle is a very good tool to explain why some individuals decide to engage in fraud and others not," he said. "The fraud triangle states three factors are normally at play for an honest person to commit fraud. There need to be opportunities, for instance weak controls. Secondly, there needs to be a motivation for the individual, for instance pressure for money, or a perceived pressure for money. And thirdly and finally, there has to be some type of rationalization a previously honest individual uses to justify to him or herself what he or she is doing, isn't wrong," Saiti explained.

The fraud triangle was developed by behavioral scientists Edwin Sutherland and Donald Cressey in the late 1970s.[25] Their theory states in short that honest individuals normally can resist engaging in fraud, but due to a combination of factors, they may sometimes not be able to resist the temptations.

According to Saiti, managers can use the fraud triangle to be more observant of when fraud and corruption might impact a company. "For instance, in times of retrenchment and uncertainty, like now in 2020 during the COVID-19 pandemic, we normally see an increase in fraudulent

25   Joseph W. Koletar et al., *A.B.C.'s of Behavioral Forensics: Applying Psychology to Financial Fraud Prevention and Detection* (New York: Wiley, 2013), chapter 3. Kindle.

activity. Employees are worried of getting fired, there might be more opportunities because of new and sudden procedures, and they might rationalize a theft with thinking they will be fired anyway," Saiti said.

If I applied the fraud triangle to understand the cement workers, I could argue the maintenance and dispatching workers who were in dire need of money, and whose job was to carry out the cement and clean up, had found an opportunity to steal cement unnoticed. The management had either not discovered the possibility, or they did not care enough to stop it. When the management didn't notice the cement workers were stealing, it became, with time, even easier for the workers to rationalize they weren't really doing anything wrong. The company didn't appear to be hurt by it.

Saiti's explanation of the fraud triangle made me think about the fraud scheme in Atsoko I discussed in the last chapter. The sales attendants had taken the opportunity thanks to our lack of oversight. Their motivation was probably also financial pressure. Even though we paid them much more than two dollars per day, our sales staff had no social security nets, and the financial pressure points could change quickly in their lives if they or a close relative got sick, for instance. But to actually cross the line and steal, the last piece of the fraud triangle was needed: rationalization. In this case, the young lady who was the instigator of the fraud had a strained relationship with the new store manager. She was spiteful and might have seen the fraud as a payback. The other sales attendants who tagged along one after another could justify the fraud with a "everyone else is doing it" rationale.

Perhaps if I would have known about the fraud triangle then, I could have kept an extra eye on the sales attendant who was unhappy before she'd been able to spread her bad behavior to the others.

* * *

If financial pressure is a common motivation for low-wage staff, what motivates the rich and powerful to engage in fraud?

Saiti has seen the rate of senior management fraud increase steadily in East Africa over the course of his career and said a perceived pressure to sustain a certain lifestyle or the responsibilities to take care of an extended family could be a motivation for senior management.

Recent behavioral research argues other motivations, such as playfulness, a need for mastery and rebelliousness, or a simple quest for thrill and danger can be other motivations for fraud when financial pressure is no longer the key driver.[26]

IT'S NOT ALWAYS ABOUT THE MONEY

I wanted to dig deeper into understanding senior management fraud, so I called up Mario Pereira, who I knew from my early career in the global telecom sector. For the last thirty years, Pereira has worked as an internal auditor with fraud investigation and fraud prevention for several companies in the telecommunication industry, spending a majority of his time in emerging markets.

---

26 Ibid.

I interviewed him over FaceTime from his home. We had not met for ten years, but his stories took me back to my early career as we gossiped for a bit about former colleagues.

Pereira used to sit across from me at the company's head office. He was a rather quiet man, with a dark humor and inquisitive eyes, who kept track of all high-risk individuals in the company. It was hardly a coincidence he sat ear-to-ear with my colleagues and I in the global procurement team. Procurement fraud was one of the most common types of fraud in the company.

I asked him if he had some examples of fraud among senior management to help me understand internal fraud.

"To give you a good example, I will tell you about this big scam when pre-paid charging platforms were rudimentary. Let's call the company Changa to protect the innocent," Pereira said. "Due to the financial situation of the company, all bonuses for management were cut that year. Then part of Changa's management team decided helping themselves to company funds. The scam was only discovered when the expat CEO and CTO eventually were fired because of performance issues. The replacement CEO who came in had the joy of discovering that the weekly company revenue instantly increased by about two hundred thousand dollars per week."

Pereira explained that the CEO and the CTO had been running a parallel business selling discounted airtime on the side after having inserted a small script on the pre-paid platform. This script allowed a subscriber's pre-paid account to be topped up, and the transaction details to be immediately scrubbed from the platform. From the pre-paid platform perspective, it was as if the transaction had never occurred. The revenues were never included in the company's income statement as the transactions were "non-existent." The script could only be accessed with the CTO's login details. A scheme like this could only be done with the collusion of C-level staff, as they were overriding all system controls in place.

I asked Pereira what happened to the CEO and the CTO.

"A case was brought against the CEO and CTO, but yet to this day, some twenty-odd years later, it has not been resolved by the local judiciary system, he said. I believe the CEO settled there, as I know he had bought some land. He was also quite a prominent person on the local social club scene and in expat circles."

"So, what do you think motivated the CEO and his CTO to do this?" I asked Pereira.

"In this case it was no longer financial pressure, as normal people know it, these guys were very well paid," Pereira said. "It could be some perceived financial pressure, as they had already committed themselves to certain luxury assets and had to compensate for their bonus loss. But I think, for the CEO especially, it was also a way to show that he was in control and superior. He had a general attitude of entitlement and disrespect for rules," Pereira continued.

* * *

Pereira had gotten the steam up and continued to tell me about another elegant fraud, this time committed by the

Chief Switch Engineer. "Let's call the operation Zynga this time, not to expose anyone," Pereira said.

"One of our competitors had noticed a call booth operator in the market was offering international calls at half the rate we and they did, so they hired some private detectives to find out what was happening," Pereira said. "The fraudster could only do this scam by free-riding one or more of the existing telecom networks there."

"It turned out that it was our network and our chief switch engineer, a very gentle and sweet man in his late fifties. He was a profoundly religious man and a prominent person in the local church. Who would have guessed he was the mastermind of such a big fraud?" Pereira said.

Pereira explained after much analytical and forensic work at the design laboratories of the supplier of the switch, they discovered Zynga's switch engineer had somehow managed to rig the switch to accept international calls to and from some international SIM cards issued by a European telecom operator. This way, he was bypassing both roaming protocols and the company's own billing systems and was even able to bypass the internal revenue assurance controls too. The switch supplier's design team had never imagined this scenario was technically feasible at that time.

Zynga's switch engineer then set up physical calling booths with phones equipped with the international SIM cards, selling discounted international calls and routing them via the company's network.

The call booth operators swiftly escaped and disappeared when the scam was discovered.

The motivation for the switch engineer to set up the scam is still unknown to Pereira. "He was also well paid, but perhaps this was a way to put away money as a nest egg for retirement," Pereira suggested.

The switch engineer was fired, and charges were put against the man. But, again this time the local judiciary system didn't work efficiently to punish the fraudster, nor did his social status change.

"One would have thought the guy, who was such a religious figure in his community, would have fallen from grace, but no," said Pereira. He continued, "Some years later, I was visiting the operation and by coincidence, I saw the guy at a Sunday church service. He was standing at the entrance of the church yard, shaking hands with everyone like a celebrity. He was obviously still very socially accepted in his community. Perhaps the community did not know about his participation in the fraud, or didn't care"

CONCLUSIONS

Internal fraud is an interesting crime to study in order to understand the forces at play in the head of a previously honest person who becomes corrupt.

My key lesson is this: the corporate world offers a range of temptations for employees and managers. According to behavioral scientists like Ariely, we are all tempted by the benefits that dishonesty can bring, but our desire to be good and honest people will normally whip us in line. The fraud triangle can help us to better understand when and why the temptation sometimes get too strong to resist. For a person to engage in fraud, there needs to be a good opportunity and a clear pressure or motivation for the employee to take the risk. Finally, if the employee is then also able to justify why it isn't wrong to commit a fraud, he or she will feel less bad about it.

With a better understanding of what motivates people to engage in fraud, managers who know their employees well can better detect staff at risk to engage in fraud.

A manager for low-wage staff needs to consider if any staff is in an acute situation of financial pressure. In an emerging market where there is no concept of the "nuclear" family, one person often supports several people in their extended family. If you understand this, you can gain some insight into their challenges. Just like government officials, they will also struggle during certain periods of the month and certain periods of the year. Every January, I had employees asking for a loan, which they then paid off during the year. What can the company do and afford? Can the company offer better safety nets, increase salaries, or offer financing options?

A manager for high-wage staff will have more complex motivations and rationalizations to analyze. Based on common motivations and rationalization discovered among employees, behavioral scientists have listed certain behavioral red flags that employees who engage in fraud may display. The below list is helpful for managers to assess motivations for fraud among more senior staff:[27,28]

1. Does your employee have new financial difficulties which can create sudden pressure to commit fraud?

27 Ibid.
28 Tracy Coenen, "How to Detect Behavioral Red Flags of Fraud," *Fraud Files Forensic Accounting Blog*, Sequence Inc, published on 12 April, 2016

2. Does your employee have any (new) family problems that put a strain on the private economy?

3. Does your employee seem to live beyond his or her means? Does he or she suddenly seem to spend more, as seen in getting a new car, a new watch, or new jewelry?

4. Does your employee show excessive control issues or an unwillingness to share duties and information? Does your employee never take his or her annual leave, is always there after hours, and would come to work even on his or her deathbed? Someone who is trying to cover their tracks will not want others to see what they do.

5. Does your employee have a poor work performance which shows he or she is unhappy or doesn't care so much about their work anymore?

6. Does your employee show unhappiness with his or her work and shows it openly?

7. Does your employee have an unusually close association with a vendor or a customer which could be a sign of kickbacks or other corrupt transactions?

8. Does your employee have a general "wheeler-dealer" attitude, and is he or she bad at respecting processes and procedures?

In the next chapter, I will dig deeper into the rationalizations people use to excuse their corrupt behavior to themselves. Rationalizations are important because they help to spread corrupt behavior. A good excuse used by one employee can become the truth for an organization. I will tell the story of Charlotte, the corporate employee who was blacklisted by the World Bank and lost her job after paying a bribe in an international aid project.

CHAPTER 3

DON'T LIE TO YOURSELF

"What happens when you come to an environment where the leader is corrupt? How quickly do you change?"

Professor Dan Ariely at Duke University, who I mentioned in the last chapter, wanted to look into this and designed an experiment which he conducted with undergraduate students at Duke.[29]

The students were invited to do a test where they would get paid depending on performance. However, depending on which group they were placed in, they could make anywhere from four dollars to forty dollars. The decision of whether they would be put in the four-dollar or forty-dollar group was made by the flip of a coin.

What the students didn't know was that the coin was rigged, so everyone was placed in the four-dollar-group. But the test leader then, after looking over his shoulder, offered each student to be placed in the forty-dollar group if the student paid him a bribe of three dollars.

---

29 *London Real TV,* "The Corruption Test - Dan Ariely," posted March 30, 2018, YouTube video, 4:45.

How many of the students paid the bribe when offered to make forty dollars instead of four dollars? According to Ariely, 90 percent.

The experiment showed a person very quickly adapts and pays a bribe in corrupt environment, and especially if the leader is corrupt. "It is very easy to corrupt people," Ariely concluded.

PAYING A BRIBE

To understand what happens with a person that works for a company where bribery is business as usual, I will tell you about Charlotte. I interviewed her over Zoom. She called in from her kitchen, and in the background, I could see photographs and notes posted on her fridge. The coffee machine was on. She looked like a normal, middle-aged, white European woman with short-cut hair and glasses. She was wearing a white cardigan over a blouse. Had this woman really been blacklisted by the World Bank for corruption?

Charlotte's employer was a small firm working as consultants for development projects mainly in Asia and Africa. Normally, the World Bank or the Asian Development Bank financed their projects. Charlotte started as a project administrator at the company in 2008 and enjoyed her work. She got to travel a lot, and she believed in the work the firm did. She worked hard, and in early 2013, she was unexpectedly promoted to director of operations in South and Southeast Asia. She felt flattered to be given this responsibility, but she was also stressed since she'd not been released from her old assignments. Suddenly she had too many parallel projects to monitor across several countries. Charlotte worked even harder—keen to deliver.

One of her new assignments was a consultation project in Southeast Asia which had gone severely off track before she became director. Charlotte went to visit the local office in Southeast Asia in February to understand what had gone wrong. Soon it became clear that Charlotte's company had won the contract based on far too small of a budget. It would be hard for her company to deliver the project without severe losses.

Charlotte tried to save the project by cutting costs and redoing the budget. When she felt ready, she finally flew back to the local office to kick off the project. It was then end of July in 2013. But new problems had arisen. The leasing fees for transport were well above what Charlotte had projected in her new budget, and the local car rental agencies were all far too expensive. The project stood idle without transportation.

Then, their local partner company approached Charlotte with a solution. The local partner could take over her transportation budget and solve all of her transportation issues. Their proposal wasn't cheap, but it was slightly better than the rental option. Charlotte did not feel comfortable with transferring a part of the budget to the local partner just like that. She made a call to her manager and asked if it was really a good idea to transfer money to the local partner for transportation. His response was: "That is nothing strange, we let our local partners handle the transport in our projects all the time." Charlotte raised her concern about the excessive amount, but again she was told to go ahead.

tated for a few more days, but as her visit started coming to an end, the local partner pushed her more and more aggressively to accept their offer. The director of the local ministry responsible for the project also reached out to push her to give the local partner the transportation budget and to not delay the project anymore.

Charlotte just wanted to go home. She had lots of other projects and problems waiting for her, so she couldn't extend her stay. She finally agreed to transfer the transportation budget to the local partner and drafted a contract, but she was not happy. The deal meant the project would hardly make any profit.

"'I've asked myself so many times why I didn't just go with the rental car option," she said. "I did have a feeling that something was very wrong with the local partner's offer."

To release some frustration, she wrote an e-mail to her colleague which would later incriminate her and be used as evidence by the World Bank for her complicity. In the e-mail to her colleague, Charlotte wrote: *"He [in reference to the local government official] will get his car that he has been pushing for, so he should be happy. A damn large portion of the budget went there."*

According to Charlotte, she didn't have any proof about the car when she wrote that e-mail. At the time, she just suspected the local partner and the government official had some deal and needed to rant about it with someone. Unfortunately for Charlotte, her nagging feeling was correct. The local partner used the transportation budget to buy a brand-new SUV for the government official.

As she got to the airport gate that night, she was exhausted and started crying out of fatigue and frustration. Then, she quickly tried to forget about what had happened and steadily continued her work at the company.

Some years later, a disgruntled consultant in the project tipped off the World Bank about the potential deal between the local partner and the director at the local ministry. The World Bank started an investigation in 2015, and three years later, in 2018, four World Bank investigators came to interrogate Charlotte at her office. They found out the director at the ministry had indeed gotten a car. And they found the e-mail sent from Charlotte to her colleague in 2013, indicating Charlotte had known about the deal.

"We were sitting in a conference room. It was surreal, like an American crime movie. The investigators all sat across from me in the room with cameras directed at me and tons of documents," Charlotte described the interrogation.

The same evening, her company sent her to another Southern Asian country to follow up on another project. The day after she had landed, she went with some local colleagues to a jewelry store. "They went there to buy a gift for the daughter of a high government official who was getting married," Charlotte said. "Their internal discussion was not about the bribe, but about how the expenses should be booked. For them it was just business as usual," she said, and shook her head.

Eventually the verdict from the World Bank investigation came. Charlotte and her employer were blacklisted from participating in any tenders funded by the development banks for three years. The local partner company was also blacklisted. However, the World Bank never targeted the local government official—something that Charlotte found somewhat odd.

JUSTIFYING CORRUPTION

What is happening here? If Charlotte thought something was funny about the transport deal, why didn't she follow up on it later? And why didn't she object to the other bribery she saw in her company?

Behavioral scientists Anand et al. have written an excellent article explaining how employees are socialized into corruption in different organizations.[30] They argue in their article that employees and managers may often have to make quick decisions based on incomplete information and under pressure, just like Charlotte. When the employees afterwards realize they have made a bad decision, they use different types of justifications to defend or excuse their behavior. Below are some common rationalizations that employees invent.[31]

Denial of Responsibility is when individuals convince themselves they are participating in corrupt acts because of circumstances; they have no real choice. Charlotte said several times during the interview the project had "ended up in her lap, and was already off track when she got it." She also said the deal between the local partner

---

30 Vikas Anand et al., "Business as usual: The acceptance and perpetuation of corruption in organizations," *Academy of Management Executive*, 18, No. 2, (2004): 39-53.

31 Ibid, pages 41-44.

and the director of the ministry must have been there before she came. Finally, she said her manager refused to listen to her concerns.

Denial of Injury is when individuals tell themselves no one is really harmed by their actions, and therefore, their actions are not really corrupt. This could, for instance, be the cement workers at the plant in the last chapter who thought their small petty pilferage wasn't really hurting their large employer. Also, the students at Duke might have used this excuse, since they could argue the test was just a test; it wasn't real life, and no one would really suffer if they paid the bribe.

Denial of Victim is when individuals think a victim deserves it. Specifically, this refers to when a theft or fraud is seen as a form of revenge. This is probably what the sales attendant at Atsoko told herself, since she disliked the new store manager.

Social Weighting is when a corrupt person defends him or herself by saying the system is unfair anyway. Social weighting was a common excuse in Tanzania for both individual and businesses to circumvent rules and regulations they thought were corrupt.

Appeal to Higher Loyalties is when employees or companies argue the higher goal justify the means. This form of rationalization is very strong, as it transforms harmful practices into worthy ones. Charlotte may also have used this rationalization. She believed that her company was doing good work. Wasn't it better to solve the problems and move on rather than cancelling the project?

Balancing the ledger is another type of common rationalization when the employee believes good work gives credit to do something corrupt. For instance, a worker who works a lot of unpaid overtime hours might justify using the company phone for personal use, just to balance out the ledger.

Do you recognize yourself in any of the above situations?

HOW CORRUPTION SPREADS

According to Anand et al., a rationalization, once successfully done, makes future wrongdoing easier, since an employee can use the same rationalization again and again.[32] Moreover, a good excuse used by an employee, and especially if used by a leader within the organization, can also be adopted by others in the organization and then spread within a group. Let's go back to Charlotte's story to see what rationalization she may have adopted.

I asked Charlotte how her colleagues and managers talked about bribery, as it must have been identified as a risk for them considering the markets and industries they were in.

"We never talked about it," Charlotte said.

While bribery was never talked about openly, Charlotte often overheard conversations among the finance team on how certain transactions should be booked. "Our business controller even had an expression for it, she called it 'funny money,'" Charlotte explained.

---

32   Ibid, page 41.

Charlotte remembered a discussion about a bill for some rental houses in a project, which were not required but the company paid for. "Everyone implicitly knew the bill for these houses was a way of paying bribes, but it was talked about as a 'business deal,' never openly as a bribe," Charlotte, said. She continued: "Everyone must have known about the bribery going on. The CFO of the company knew about those houses, for example, and she was in the management team," Charlotte said.

When I pressured her again on why she hadn't objected to the transportation transaction, Charlotte said she felt employees who were flexible and pragmatic were rewarded, while employees who were seen as problematic were bad-mouthed. Charlotte recalled how a female colleague of hers based in Nairobi, who had a very clear stance against corruption, was described by colleagues and management as competent, but too rigid. The office in Nairobi finally had to close down as the company had not managed to win a single contract there. Among Charlotte's colleagues and the management, it was understood the failure was due to Charlotte's female colleague, who had been "too inflexible" and not made any "business deals."

In short, Charlotte's company justified the bribes as an appeal to higher loyalties and social weighting. If they didn't pay the bribes, they would lose the contracts to other companies who did. Colleagues and managers at the head office, even managers at the highest level, seemed to have accepted these excuses; no one objected. Their silence blessed the corruption to continue.

* * *

The spread of what is rationalized as acceptable behavior among several individuals is done through methods of socialization. According to Anand et al., a successful socialization makes a newcomer feel he or she is making the decision to join a certain activity voluntarily and is not being forced into it.[33] Charlotte was never told directly to pay a bribe. She was just never explicitly told *not* to pay a bribe.

Lighter terms like "business deal" were used instead of the more offensive "bribe." This practice of using light terms to talk about corrupt acts is another common way to normalize corruption. This is called the use of euphemistic language.[34] A "business deal" and "funny money" sound much less offensive than "bribe," and "flexible and pragmatic" sounds much better than "corrupt." I experienced the use of these light terms in Tanzania all the time. A customs agent or a police officer would never ask for a bribe, but they would instead ask for some soda money or simply a tea. If an official asked for larger bribes, he or she would ask for some "help" and talk about how high the school fees were for his or her kids.

Anand et al. lists three common methods for the effective socialization of a newcomer into corrupt behavior.[35]

Incrementalism means the newcomer is induced to small acts of corruption, step by step. Over the years, Charlotte

---

33 Ibid, page 45.

34 Ibid, page 47.

35 Ibid, pages 41-44.

had seen and not objected to the common practices in the company of covering up bribery. Charlotte heard her colleagues justify the bribery with a mentality that ends always justify means. As the individual comes to accept these small, corrupt acts as normal, he or she becomes complicit in a way and may be susceptible to try other, more corrupt acts.

Co-optation means rewards or power are used to attract individuals to join in on corrupt practices. An employee is rewarded if he or she follows the rule of the game. When Charlotte was promoted, she felt flattered for being given the responsibility and wanted to prove she was worthy. She also remembered the colleague who had been considered as too rigid and didn't win any business.

Compromise is the third form of socialization, linked to the rationale of the end justifying the means. Charlotte's company had to compromise some of their integrity for the greater good, and the same applied for their employees.

In short, Charlotte was subject to all three methods of socialization in her company, and so she became responsible, together with her colleagues and managers, for allowing corruption to continue.

CONCLUSIONS

Rationalization and socialization explain why honest employees and managers accept corrupt practices they wouldn't find acceptable otherwise.

By understanding how rationalization and socialization work, both employees and managers can become more alert to their reactions when exposed to corrupt behavior.

What I found especially intriguing when interviewing Charlotte was I never heard her take any responsibility for the corruption going on in her company. She was obviously an honest person who worked with international aid because she believed in helping others, so why did she accept the corruption happening in her organization without objections? Could it be she'd adopted the rationalizations used in her company so strongly that, after some time, she also thought the bribes were necessary "business deals?" And was she, perhaps, afraid of losing her job and the colleagues who had become her friends if she made trouble?

Rationalizations, when done well like in Charlotte's example, can blind us to the truth and to our own complicity. In the next chapter, I will expound on this phenomenon called "wishful blindness." I will tell the story of a man who was defrauded by his wife for years and refused to see it, nor did he ask any questions. Love can make us blind.

CHAPTER 4

OPEN YOUR EYES

Why did Charlotte and her colleagues not see their own roles and responsibilities in the corruption going on in their company? All employees were highly educated people working in the international aid sector. They knew corruption was wrong, but they decided not to talk about it, not to see it, nor to admit their own responsibility and involvement.

The legal term for this is called willful ignorance. The term used by behavioral scientists is "willful blindness." Professor and blogger Margaret Heffernan has written a book on the topic titled *Willful Blindness: Why We Ignore the Obvious at Our Peril.*[36] Behavioral scientists argue our brain is not able to handle too many conflicting interests or emotions, and therefore decides to block out what disturbs us. Our brain makes us partially blind to help us cope. The same mechanisms support our rationalizations of corrupt acts described in the previous chapter. A person who does not want to take responsibility for something may lie to him

---

36 Margaret Heffernan, *Willful Blindness: Why We Ignore the Obvious at Our Peril* (London: Simon & Schuster, 2011), Introduction. Kindle.

or herself and often disregard or refuse to see the facts and arguments to avoid facing the truth.[37]

Willful blindness is relevant to understanding fraud and corruption because it explains what makes owners, managers, and employees ignore the crimes happening in their businesses.

LOVE IS BLIND

One of the most heartbreaking stories I heard when researching this book is a story of willful blindness in a family business in Tanzania.

The narrator of this story is Joyce, though that is not her real name. Joyce is one of the individuals who became very important to me in Tanzania as one of my tax advisors. Over the years, she also became my friend and my tax therapist. She would laugh with me—and at me—giving emotional and moral support while I bounced all my tax issues with her. She is also a complete nerd when it comes to Tanzanian tax law.

When I interviewed her for this book, Joyce was sitting in her small office on the outskirts of Dar es Salaam. Her office building had finally been finished, and the noisy construction work had come to an end. Building material, equipment, and tools were, however, still scattered on the ground around the building. Joyce was looking at the mess right outside her window as she started telling me the story of Tom and his construction business.

"Tom was a friend of a friend who asked for my help with cleaning up his family business," Joyce started the story.

37   Ariely, *The (Honest) Truth About Dishonesty,* Introduction.

Tom's business had expanded quickly, and he realized the informal way he had been running the business was no longer sustainable. Tom had started out a small business together with his wife, leasing construction equipment and machinery mainly to private customers. Tom contacted Joyce as the company was getting bigger, getting more and more requests from corporate customers wanting to lease construction equipment. These customers required proper receipts and invoices. Tom wanted to grow with them.

"No problem," Joyce had said. "I will help you out." Joyce had just started her own advisory firm together with a colleague and offered tax advisory, accounting, and auditing services. Both Joyce and her colleague had worked at global accounting firms in the region and had extensive experience in cleaning up companies.

But Tom's business became one of the most disturbing fraud stories Joyce had seen throughout her career.

"When family members steal from each other, that is the most shocking to me." Joyce can't stop herself from laughing from the darkness of the story, and the phone rattles as she shakes her head in disbelief and clicks her tongue.

It started off badly. Tom's wife, a powerful-looking woman with exclusive Brazilian hair weaves and long manicured nails on both fingers and toes, was not keen on letting Joyce clean up her business. She simply refused to give Joyce and the audit team access to her accounting books.

"The wife was handling all the private customers of the business who were still an important part of the business," Joyce explained. 'The wife was also responsible for the sale of building material to the smaller private customers. The wife's business was mainly cash based."

"I got suspicious because the wife didn't want anyone to touch her records. She was angry as a lion and would blast off our accountant," Joyce said. Joyce couldn't glean any insight into the wife's business in any way, as the wife received all orders on her phone and handled the lease and sales in cash. Unless the wife recorded the sale, no one else in the company would know. There was no way for Joyce to reconcile transactions.

The wife looked like a big, red flag of fraud to Joyce, who had learned to recognize fraudulent behavior: the wife's unwillingness to share information, her defensiveness when she was questioned, and the complete lack of internal controls. Joyce decided to look into the wife's personal assets. "That is when we noticed the wife owned some houses," Joyce said.

Joyce approached Tom and told him carefully about the difficulties with getting information from his wife and the risks with the wife's informal business processes. Tom laughed a bit nervously but wasn't able to help much. It was clear Tom did not want to confront his wife. "When we asked Tom about his wife's funds, Tom told me that he had tried to ask his wife where all her money came from. But she had told him the money came from her family. He had left it at that, as he didn't want to create any arguments," Joyce said.

There were lots of reasons for Tom to ask Joyce to look into his wife's business, but he decided not to. Instead he focused on cleaning up his own side of the business, and Joyce helped him with that. The strategy worked well. "When we started working with Tom's side of the business, the revenue was fifteen to thirty million [fifteen thousand US dollars], now they have a turnover of two billion [one million US dollars]," Joyce said. The wife's part of the business has slowed down, and the wife has been less and less active in the business."

When Tom got older and wanted to hand over the business, Joyce and her team helped him set up a board and groom a team to take over both the accounting department and the general manager role. "Then we could finally also remove the wife from the operations," Joyce said with a more content laugh.

WHAT MAKES US BLIND

What happened to Tom? Why didn't he confront his wife? Heffernan would have argued he was blinded by love. She writes, "Nations, institutions, individuals can all be blinded by love, by the need to believe themselves good and worthy and valued."[38] Emotions like guilt, shame, and hurt can be hard to deal with, and our brain can help us avoid these feelings. In order to protect both his own feelings and his marriage, Tom closed his eyes to his wife's potential fraud.

What other human weaknesses can blind us? Behavioral scientists have looked into this.

Our wish to belong to a group and our tendency to blindly follow a charismatic (and sometimes evil) authority are

---

38 Heffernan, *Willful Blindness,* chapter 2.

well known examples of willful blindness. Throughout history, we have seen several examples of when obedience is directly linked to evil acts committed by otherwise decent people. The Nazi movement is a strong example of this phenomenon which I don't think I need to develop in this book. A good book focused on the specific topic of how certain social environments of authority create evil is *The Lucifer Effect: How Good People Turn Evil*.[39] Examples from the corporate world are, for instance, the Theranos case or the Enron case, where charismatic leaders managed to make both employees and investors accept a distorted reality.[40, 41]

Conflicts of interests may be yet another reason for our brain to block out one interest for another and as well as the feelings associated. Corporate environments are full of conflicts of interest for employees and manager: the conflicts between profit and ethics, between personal gain and company interest, and the promotion of others and promotion of self. Behavioral economist Ariely describes how these conflicts of interests are really hard for us to manage. We will fall falter sooner or later and choose the interest that suits us best, not necessarily what is morally right.[42]

Further, Ariely argues too many temptations put in front of us day after day can also deplete our willpower. Behavioral scientists call this ego depletion. We can't say no to

---

39 Philip Zimbardo, The Lucifer Effect: How Good People Turn Evil (London: Random House, 2009).

40 *Encyclopaedia Britannica Online, Academic ed.* s.v., "Elizabeth Holmes," accessed September 21, 2020.

41 *Encyclopaedia Britannica Online*, Peter Bondarenko. s.v., "Enron scandal," accessed September 21, 2020.

42 Ariely, *The (Honest) Truth About Dishonesty*, chapter 3.

ourselves for too long. When we overcompensate and are too good in one area, we have to give in to another area.[43] This ego depletion explains why I always need a glass of wine, or a couple of glasses of wine, after a long day.

We shouldn't underestimate fatigue as a factor in willful blindness and potential participation in acts of corruption. Heffernan argues, besides making us less effective in seeing warning signals, fatigue can also restrict our moral engagement. As an example, she gives the American soldier who was sentenced for abusing inmates at Abu Ghraib in Iraq. He was found to have worked twelve-hour shifts seven days a week, with few days off. He was also "surrounded by colleagues just as ill-trained and just as exhausted," the author says, which "meant no one was awake enough to have any moral sensibility left."[44]

Ariely makes a more relatable example of how fatigue can corrupt us. He gives the simple example of how we, when tired and exhausted, in most cases, would go for a greasy pizza rather than a boring salad—despite knowing the pizza won't be good for us. This is linked to the human-old conflict between desire and reason. When the part of your brain normally handling reason is too busy or too tired, your desires take over.[45] I think the customs and immigration officials in Tanzania knew this intuitively. More often, their requests would come on a Friday afternoon when I was exhausted and just wanted to go home rather than on a Tuesday morning when I was fit for a fight.

---

43 Ariely, *The (Honest) Truth About Dishonesty*, chapter 4.

44 Heffernan, *Willful Blindness*, chapter 4.

45 Ariely, *The (Honest) Truth About Dishonesty*, chapter 4.

Distance is another mechanism we use to block things out. What we don't see, doesn't exist. To manage the problem with the wife, Tom and Joyce intentionally isolated the wife's business, instead focusing on growing Tom's side of the business. This strategy can successfully be implemented in larger businesses as well. The CEO who removes him of herself physically from the ground can more easily turn a blind eye to dirty things going on there. A company outsourcing the hard things to subcontractors is also using the same mechanism of distance. People using euphemisms and numbers are distancing themselves. Distance reduces guilt.[46]

THE RUSSIAN LAUNDROMAT

Swedbank, one of the oldest and most reputable banks in Scandinavia, is an example of a company that walked into a high-risk market with their eyes (willfully) closed. The bank became a laundromat for Russian oligarchs who, during more than a decade, washed hundreds of millions of dirty euros through Swedbank.

An hour-long exposé on Swedish Public Television, called "Uppdrag Granskning" tells us the facts of the story I will retell below.[47]

The laundromat business started when Swedbank entered the Baltics around 2007. Banking institutions in the Baltics had by then already been used by oligarchs and the Russian mafia for years to move illegal funds

---

46 London Real TV "The Corruption Test."

47 *Swedish Public Television (SVT),* Uppdrag granskning, "Swedbank och penningtvätten," TV-program, posted on April 15, 2020.

from the former Soviet states to Europe, the US, and to tax havens. Swedbank knew this when they entered the market, but they reasoned they were a retail bank focused only on local retail clients and local businesses, so they could avoid engaging with risky clients and the risks of money laundering. However, bank employees at the local Swedbank branches somehow managed to circumvent the systems set up for to prevent money laundering and pursued business with high-risk clients against the internal rules.[48]

The money laundering became public in 2019, thanks to a whistleblower who leaked internal transaction documents from the bank to some Swedish investigative journalists.

To analyze the data, the journalists used common red flags for money laundering. The journalists looked, for instance, for so-called "company mills" that offer shady businesses a seemingly reputable address. On one occasion they found one thousand and two hundred Swedbank clients all registered with the same UK address. They crosschecked the company names of these suspicious addresses against blacklists from, for instance, Transparency International. Quickly, they found companies linked to the Russian mafia, the Magnitsky case, Viktor Yanukovych—the former disgraced president of Ukraine—and Mossack Fonseca, the law firm at the epicenter of the Panama Papers scandal.[49] Just to exemplify the gravity of these cases, the Magnitsky case refers to the Russian lawyer Sergei Magnitsky who investigated and revealed a large tax fraud scheme involving Russian

48 Ibid.
49 Ibid.

public officials. He was arrested in Russia and then died in prison at thirty-seven years old. The US passed the Magnitsky Act following his death, issuing sanctions against the individual Russian officials involved, including freezing of their bank accounts and assets abroad.[50] According to Uppdrag Granskning, some of the money laundered through Swedbank came from the Russian public officials involved.[51]

During the following investigation, it became clear Swedbank's board and CEO had been given several warning signals of potential money laundering in the Baltics but failed to act on them. For instance, in 2017, their competitor, Danske Bank, was accused and found guilty for money laundering in Estonia. When questioned in the media, the CEO for Swedbank, Birgitte Bonnesen, repeatedly claimed there was no risk that Swedbank was involved in money laundering. Swedbank had a zero-tolerance policy against money laundering and did not deal with this type of high-risk clients. Later, in 2019, when confronted with the evidence Swedbank had indeed made transactions with the same type of criminal clients found at Danske Bank, she was speechless.[52]

How could the CEO not have seen this? When it was so easy for outsiders to see what was happening, it is hard to for me to believe that the board and the bank management didn't see the large money flows going through the Baltics. Was it all just a slippery slope they fell down?

50 Roman Goncharenko, "Magnitsky a symbol of sanctions — and not just in Russia," *Deutsche Welle*, November 16, 2019.

51 *SVT*, Uppdrag granskning, 2020.

52 Ibid.

Did they see the benefits of this line of business and then couldn't stop themselves from pursuing them? Were the profits too good, or were they afraid they would get too many questions to answer if the money flow suddenly stopped? They consciously or unconsciously closed their eyes—not to be disturbed by the problem.

Bonnesen and the board were fired after the scandal became public. Swedbank's new board and management hired a leading law firm, Clifford Chance, and forensic auditing firm FTI consulting to dig out what happened and clean it up. The very damning report was presented just before the COVID-19 breakout in March 2020 and showed Swedbank had, without doubt, inadequate internal controls. Thousands of clients should never have been allowed to bank with Swedbank. Swedbank was fined four hundred million dollars under the Swedish anti-terrorism and anti-money-laundering acts.[53] Bonnesen is currently being investigated for fraud because of her public statements declaring Swedbank did not have any potential money laundering issues.[54]

In researching this case, I spoke with Sina Bahrami, who has been following the Swedbank affair closely, since he was a part of the forensic audit team hired by Swedbank. Bahrami has worked most of his career in forensic auditing.

According to Bahrami, the money laundering happened partly because the leadership team sitting in Stockholm

53   Ibid.
54   Jan Almgren, "Utredning mot Bonnesen växer – åtal närmar sig," Svenska Dagbladet, August 24, 2020.

had not been present and not in control of what happened in the Baltics. "The management thought they could apply the same level of internal regulatory controls in the Baltics they had been applying in Sweden. You can claim ignorance, but only to a point," Bahrami said. He continued, "In an industry like the banking industry in the Baltics, which was already known to be a resort for money laundering, you have a duty as management to be present. You need to be there and understand what they are doing. In any banking environment where you may have clients who acquired their wealth in questionable ways and who deal with poorly paid bank employees, the risk of fraud, corruption, and money laundering becomes high. Especially if the bank employees are also incentivized based on new business they bring in and have no incentives to perform proper due diligence on new clients. It's a pattern we see all the time in the investigations we do."

The bank management had chosen to distance themselves and closed their eyes.

CONCLUSIONS

Heffernan argues that willful blindness is damaging. "We make ourselves powerless when we pretend we don't know. That's the paradox of blindness: we think it will make us safe even as it puts us in danger."[55]

Willful ignorance can hurt society, as we have seen in this chapter. Bahrami described the money laundering by Swedbank in Baltics not just as a regulatory control failure but as a moral failure. "A large portion of the money

55   Heffernan, Willful Blindness, chapter 2.

laundered through Swedbank was misappropriated funds from Ukraine's treasury by their then president, Viktor Yanukovych, and some of it came from the infamous Magnitsky case," he said.

When a lot of people practice willful blindness for corruption, it creates a silent blessing of the corrupt act. When managers like Tom and Bonnesen practice it as leaders, they influence the rest of the organization. Who would have dared to confront Tom's wife, if not even Tom dared to? Which employees dared to question the management at Swedbank who so assertively said they had a zero-tolerance policy on money laundering? How could Charlotte, who I talked about in the previous chapter, question her manager who told her local partners managed transport budgets all the time? Managers need to be especially careful of willful blindness and be very brave to confront it.

In researching willful blindness, my admiration for whistleblowers is even higher. They should rightfully be seen as heroes because they tell uncomfortable truths.

From Heffernan's book, listed below are some main tips on how to avoid willful blindness.[56]

1. Listen to the little voice in your head telling you that something is not right. Try to become aware of what you are trying to avoid and what you can do about it. Become aware of your biases.

2. Question the truths that no one challenges.

3. Remember that it takes courage to see your own weaknesses and the weaknesses of people you love and admire.

---

56   Heffernan, Willful Blindness, chapter 12.

4. Seek objective third opinions from people. If you can't see it yourself, perhaps others can.

5. Try to avoid making morally questionable decisions when you are too tired and take some rest.

6. Encourage a culture where people dare to speak up by, for instance, incentivizing whistleblowing.

With the next chapter and second part of this book, I will start applying what we have learnt about the psychology of corruption. How can we use this knowledge to build an honest organization? In my opinion, it starts with setting the right tone at the top. I will talk about Alfonso, the corporate manager in the cement industry, who once waited two years for a permit to show that his company wouldn't pay any bribes, no matter the cost.

PART II

MANAGING FRAUDSTERS AND RACKETEERS

CHAPTER 5

HOW TO SET THE TONE

Based on my own experience and research, a fuzzy tone from the top will make it hard for an organization to maintain its integrity. The big question is, will the company really prioritize ethics over profits, no matter the cost?

The writer Samuel Richardson said already in the 1700s: "Calamity is the test of integrity." To withstand the constant calamities in a high-risk market, a tone of zero tolerance from the top needs to be implemented with tools and resources for the people on the ground. Note my message is not about the necessity of just communicating a zero-tolerance policy, but rather about the necessity of providing the required strategies and resources for achieving zero tolerance.

LESSON 1 – ANTI-CORRUPTION IS A BOARD MATTER

To get some good ideas for managers and boards on how to set up a credible anti-corruption plan, I spoke with the anti-corruption expert Philippe Montigny, founder of the company ETHIC Intelligence, an anti-corruption certification agency. He has trained many managers over the years on anti-bribery strategies. He has also worked with developing the 37001 ISO standard, the first international anti-bribery management system, offered by the International Organization for Standardization, among other things.[57]

In his book *Integrity for Competitiveness: On the Road with Compliance Officers*, Montigny writes about the importance of the board in setting a tone of anti-corruption. If the board will not support the management in their anti-corruption efforts, it will be very hard for the managers to maintain integrity.[58] When boards or investors are faced with the choice between ethics and short-term profit, leadership sentiment needs to be consistent.

It may help to remember why it is so important to say no. Besides the moral reasons, corruption is also a business risk. Montigny gave the fall and rise of Siemens as an example in our interview. The German technology company Siemens, a manufacturer of telecom, power, transport and medical equipment, paid more than $1.4 billion in bribes to government officials in Asia, Africa, Europe, the Middle East and the Americas over almost two decades.

"When Siemens was hit by a corruption scandal in 2008, it was discovered bribery was part of the business model. When the new management started a zero-tolerance policy, they realized some business areas had to be discontinued, as these business areas were no longer profitable. Why? Because bribery gave, during many

---

57 "ISO 37001 Anti-bribery-management," ISO, accessed October 12, 2020.

58 Philippe Montigny, *Integrity for Competitiveness: on the road with compliance officers* (Paris; ETHIC Intelligence Publishing, 2018).

years, the wrong information to the top management on how competitive these business areas really were. When the bribery stopped, these business areas were not competitive anymore. Siemens couldn't catch up with their competitors who, meanwhile, had been investing more in research and product development," Montigny explained.

After the corruption scandal erupted in 2008, Siemens had to pay $1.6 billion in fines to German and US authorities under the FCPA.[59]

According to Montigny, the corruption scandal was like an earthquake in Germany and within Siemens. Siemens chose to fully cooperate with the US authorities through an in-depth legal and forensic investigation in all its operations worldwide at an additional cost of $2.2 billion. Under tough monitoring by the US, Siemens then implemented a comprehensive anti-corruption compliance program run by the former German finance minister Theo Waigel. Over a year, more than six hundred anti-corruption compliance officers were hired, one hundred new corruption prevention and control processes were designed, and a yearly budget of one hundred million euros was allocated to compliance.

"Despite the heavy fines, the business restructuring, and the costly compliance program, Siemens became profitable again. Siemens has been the first example of a company demonstrating that when integrity and anti-corruption measures are properly integrated in

59 Bertrand Venard, "Lessons from the massive Siemens corruption scandal one decade later," *The Conversation*, December 13, 2018.

strategic decisions *as well as* in operations, it ensures a profitable and sustainable business," Montigny added.

Montigny gave some more practical examples of how to integrate an anti-corruption strategy with a company's strategy and operations.

"If you are committed not to pay bribes, you cannot, for instance, approve a business plan and budget based on just-in-time deliveries in a market where the custom authority is corrupt. Then you need to build up a stock to resist bribery in customs," Montigny said. "Anti-corruption will have a direct impact on a company's balance sheet, your working capital, and financing cost. Instead of a one- to two-month stock, you might need to have a four- to six-month stock. However, in doing so, you will successfully resist to extortion solicitations and build your reputation as an "incorruptible" company. And if the first years are difficult, over time this "no tolerance policy" will pay back, and your company will be less confronted by racketeering situations."

Montigny continued explaining: "Each time you accept to pay a bribe, you take an appointment for another bribe next week, or next month, or next year! But if you say no—and even if it is costly and time consuming—you break this vicious circle and open a new way of doing business."

"In the short term, saying no to corruption, will make your life very hard, and your company will most likely lose out on opportunities and short-term profit; but in the long term, it is the only sustainable solution if you want to build and grow a business, especially when operating in high-risk markets," Montigny ended.

LESSON 2 – TIME IS YOUR BEST RESOURCE AGAINST CORRUPTION

What does an anti-corruption strategy look like on the ground? How does it help you to say no to a solicitation for a bribe? I went back to Alfonso to let him share his experiences from the field.

"Firstly, I have learned how important appearance is. It's the way you behave, what you say, or what you do that will either invite people to request a bribe from you, or make them hesitate," he said. "It has actually only happened twice during all my years in Africa that I've been asked directly for a bribe."

I asked him for an example.

"As soon as you get a hint from someone, like if there's a delay of a permit or something similar, it is often a sign somebody wants something from you. Then, you just have to play naive and make them understand you are not going to pay. Let me tell you about this time when I waited two years for a permit," he said with a laugh.

The setting was a smaller sub-Saharan country; we can call the country Nebanu. Alfonso was sent there by his employer to set up and obtain all the permits for a new cement plant in 2010. A new cement plant is a huge investment, at least a two-hundred-million-dollar investment, and it will bring more than one thousand jobs for the community. "A cement plant is something you build for the long term, a fifty-year investment or more, so you need to make sure that all permits, licenses, etc. are in order before you start putting in your money," Alfonso explained.

The small town where the plant was to be built, which we can call Tobi, is a very hot, tropical, and swampy area with strong rains. The town is located a bit north of the equator. "We even had hippos roaming around the quarry," Alfonso said.

"We had spent almost one million dollars on the exploration phase, and we were waiting for a license from the local mayor in the town of Tobi. But he was delaying and delaying. At least sixty times, I got in my car, drove the one-and-a-half hours or more from our office in the main capital, and then waited for hours in that stuffy little government office with worn and dirty sofas and a noisy air conditioner. Sometimes the mayor met with me, sometimes he just let me wait," Alfonso told me.

The mayor was always nice—he smiled—but he never asked Alfonso straight-out for a bribe.

"Sometimes he would call me and say, "The permit is ready." And then I would drive there, but when I got there, he had some new excuses. I know he wanted me to ask him what he needed to get the permit issued, but I never gave him that chance," Alfonso said.

"And finally, the mayor asked to see my managers. So, the big bosses flew in to meet him. We waited in that little room—six of us, all men in suits—with only seats for four of us in those sofas. When the mayor finally met with us, he spoke to my bosses: 'You have waited here for a couple of hours. This man,' he said, as he pointed at me, 'has waited here for two years, and always with a smile.' Then, we finally got the permit," Alfonso said with another smile.

Part of the reason they got the permit was, according to Alfonso, "because they had left the door open for the mayor to do the right thing."

"Never leave a cat without an exit," Alfonso explained. "As you can't trust the legal system, always treat the public official with respect and keep a good relationship so he or she can come around. You can't let your opponent lose his or her face. Once you take a public official or a government agency to the courts, you may actually have to leave the country."

Alfonso's story and its resolution is a case study of a well-resourced manager who set a tone of zero tolerance. How different would the outcome have been had Alfonso felt the pressure from his executives to be "proactive" in order to secure the permit sooner, despite a clearly stated and well-communicated anti-corruption policy?

Montigny would have applauded Alfonso's waiting strategy. The company showed its long-term commitment and was willing to take the extra costs of saying no. In Montigny's experience, time—what Alfonso used as his tool in this case—is the best resource you can use to resist corruption, especially extortion solicitations by government officials. Lack of time and stress to meet targets are often the key reasons why managers agree to pay a bribe to fast track a permit.

To get the courage to say no to a bribe, a manager needs time, and he needs to feel sure his company is prepared to take the extra costs related to compliance and anti-bribery tactics.

LESSON 3 – REMIND YOURSELF AND OTHERS WHY YOU ARE SAYING NO

When saying no to a bribe is especially painful, you may have to remind yourself and others why you are saying no to corruption. Besides the moral reasons and the link between anti-corruption and long-term competitiveness, Montigny demonstrated with the Siemens case there are a few more strong arguments:

1. Heavy fines for the company and potential imprisonment of managers under the international anti-corruption legislations.

2. The reputational risk related to corruption may make a company a tainted asset suppliers and investors may not want to be associated with for decades to come.

On the first argument, I asked Alfonso if the tougher legislation has had any real effect on the ground. According to Alfonso, managers working for global corporates in high-risk markets have indeed become more aware of the personal risk they are taking if engaging in corruption. The headlines of huge fines have a deterring effect on mangers. Alfonso mentioned the ongoing Lafarge case as a warning example.

Lafarge and nine of its executives are currently under trial for paying at least five million euros to the IS (the

Islamic State) and other armed groups in Syria between 2012 and 2014. Lafarge have confessed their Syrian subsidiary was indeed paying armed groups for protection to be able to continue operating their factory in northeastern Syria. The Lafarge executives could face penalties of up to ten years in jail as well as fines, if prosecuted. In late 2019, Lafarge and its directors were indicted for terrorism financing, violation of embargo, and endangering the lives of their Syrian workers. The latter related to Lafarge only evacuating their expatriate staff once it was clear to them the security situation was untenable, leaving their local staff behind to a raging war. The case is currently under appeal and will likely take years to resolve.[60]

"A corporate manager for an international company should know the risk is now on him or her," said Alfonso. "The board can't protect the managers. But we still have a lot of countries that haven't really enforced these types of anti-bribery acts. And smaller companies are not as affected, so many companies and managers still don't have to care," he said.

The second argument—the risk of becoming a tainted asset—may be something for smaller local businesses to really consider. If a local business has the ambition to become a supplier or subcontractor to international companies or to raise money from international investors, they will need to be clean. Alfonso, who has worked on several due diligence cases for corporate acquisitions within the cement industry, gave several examples of local cement companies that failed the due diligence on

60 Liz Alderman, "Terrorism Financing Charge Upheld Against French Company Lafarge," *New York Times*, November 7, 2019.

compliance and therefore had not been acquired. A few of these companies were family businesses, which suddenly stood without their succession plans, since the kids did not want to take over and no serious buyer wanted to buy them as tainted asset.

LESSON 4 – MANAGE YOURSELF

How do you see your own role and responsibility as a manager when it comes to anti-bribery? Your actions will be pivotal for how your team will handle similar opportunities. Will you always say no, or will you sometimes justify a bribe as a means to a higher end? If you do accept bribes every once in a while, then be aware you will inspire your employees to do the same, and their threshold may be far lower than yours. It's a slippery slope. In the end, it is you as a manager who decides and allocates resources to set the tone.

Joyce, my tax advisor and friend, argued the lack of controls for the founders and owners is one of the key fraud issues in the local family businesses she has worked with. "A problem with many African-owned businesses is that the segregation of business and private is poor. Many African business owners don't pay themselves well from the company and instead take money from the business, and they take without any control. Employees then follow the same behavior," Joyce explained.

* * *

It is lonely at the top sometimes. If you, as a manager, want to lead by example, you need to do three things, in my opinion, to support yourself. First, identify your weaknesses—the temptations that tease you—and the rationalizations you may use. Second, limit your own opportunities to stray from your morals. Third, give yourself a break when you feel you need one.

Start with identifying your weaknesses and potential motivations. For instance, my research on rationalization helped me recognize several excuses which would run through my head when considering a solicitation for a bribe to fast-track mind-numbing regulatory processes. I could use the excuse of the ends justifying the means or that we were better than anyone else anyway. But, the real motivation for me behind those excuses was I was tired and wanted to take a shortcut to focus on other things.

Then, as a manager in a company in a corrupt environment, you need to minimize the opportunities for yourself (and potentially your board). Set up rules in your companies to keep yourself in place. Alfonso said, for instance, one thing that had helped him a lot was to set up very strict processes and procedures in the businesses he managed. Even if he would have wanted to, it was impossible for him to do anything illicit on his own. I found I used the same tactics once I had hired my management team. I set up authorization processes and procedures making it difficult for everyone in the company, including myself, to use company funds for anything odd without several people needing to know what the money was used for.

To give you an example of how my own business processes would directly hinder me from doing anything corrupt, I will describe a common invite for tax evasion: the offers from suppliers to undervalue import. Undervaluing imports is one of the most frequent types of tax crimes in emerging markets and may be tempting as "everyone is doing it," but it corrupts at the core of your trading business: your gross margin.

One of the reasons it is so common in East Africa is because import tariffs and barriers to foreign products are punitive. The goods we were selling—foreign beauty brands—carry 25 percent import duty, 10 percent excise duty, and 18 percent import value-added tax (VAT.) The proposal several suppliers, mainly smaller businesses, gave us was an offer to undervalue their goods. Undervalue means the supplier sells us a product at one price— let's say for ten dollars—but the official invoice states only five dollars. We would then save 50 percent of the import duties. In addition, clearing services costs would be lower as they are linked to the value of the shipment.

The undervalue scheme would have a direct positive effect on our income statement. However, to do it, I would have had to involve my finance team to cover up the tracks of the tax evasion. We would have to cook the books and, for instance, pay the supplier the balance through some slush funds that couldn't be seen—revenue we could have somehow managed to siphon out of the company. Having very strict processes and approval procedures in a company is obvious for larger businesses, but not so evident for many smaller businesses like Atsoko, where I, as the CEO, was the jack of all trades.

Finally, I needed to give myself a break sometimes. I couldn't always be the strong, responsible, and consistent manager. The harder I worked and the more tired I got, the higher the risk I would take short cuts. Get out, take a break, and invest in your own personal moral resilience to maintain you and your company's integrity when it matters.

CONCLUSIONS

Setting and conveying a clear tone and policy of zero tolerance from the top is one of the most important tools a company can use to resist corruption and decrease fraud in company. But it is not easy to walk the talk, since the conflict of interest between ethics and profit will always be there. A manager could consider the below as a help to keep him or herself in line.

1. A manager needs the support from the board. Saying no to corruption and fraud will have an impact on both timelines and financials and will require an aligned strategy, budget, and allocation of resources.

2. The appearance of a company and a manager being untouchable is more important than you think, as it will stop solicitations for bribes to even come to your door. By making third parties and employees see you as a manager and a board who are not prepared to compromise the values of your company, no matter the cost and time, you will make great strides in inspiring anti-corruption.

3. When it is especially hard to say no to corruption, remind yourself of the long-term costs and the huge risk of engaging in corruption. Among those are the risks of incrimination, reputational risk, and the

potential for your company to become a tainted asset no one wants to deal with.

4. It is lonely at the top. You need to set your very own strong moral compass and understand your own weaknesses. If you know you risk to stray from your morals and get tempted by opportunities, use your employees as your gate keepers and set up strict rules in the company, making it hard for you as a top manager to do anything corrupt without everyone knowing.

In the next chapter, I will talk more about how to set the tone by finding and building a good and honest team in an environment with plenty of temptations for corruption. This might sometimes require new and innovative human resource management tools. One of the things we did in Atsoko was to set up our own internal court of justice: an internal disciplinary committee run by our own employees.

CHAPTER 6

HOW TO BUILD AN HONEST TEAM

———

After having lost lots of money and many good employees to fraud during the first years of running Atsoko, I made good strides quickly once I started focusing on combating internal fraud and corruption risks. My proudest achievement today is the great team and culture I built during my last two years as a manager.

Within a year of some serious anti-fraud measures, Atsoko had pilferage below 1 percent across our seven stores, and our employee turnover rate went down significantly after as well. The biggest reason for staff turnover had previously been theft and poor performance. Better staff retention strengthened our corporate culture, which in turn kept an honest culture within the company.

Our internal controls also made our anti-corruption policy much stronger. No one could pay any amount without a proper receipt. And it also made everyone happier, as everyone knew what they were and weren't supposed to do and got rewarded for it.

LESSON 1 - GET A CORE TEAM OF GOOD PEOPLE

The silver lining to the fraudulent events in my company—described in the first chapter—was the realization I'd actually built an honest core team around me over the years. They had been as hurt as me by the frequent scams and were as keen as I was to root out bad behavior in the company. One of my male Tanzanian employees said he really felt betrayed and was so disappointed in his colleagues. We all started thinking of how we could prevent this from happening again.

Several in my core team were alumni from an international student network called AIESEC—an organization promoting youth leadership among university students and recent graduates—some of them were Tanzanian graduates, and others were international graduates. When hiring them, I looked specifically for two characteristics: team spirit and interest in working with and helping develop others. The AIESEC alumni had already been given leadership training and been exposed to the importance of team building. Once they came to Atsoko, they reinforced good values and behavior between each other. They socialized newcomers into the same culture. In addition, I had a few loyal employees who had been with me for several years and shown both good work ethics and performance. They became role models as well, showing we did invest in employees and proving it's possible to make a career within the company. Together, we started building a very distinct Atsoko culture.

Don't expand as a company if you don't feel you have a team with good values around you helping you build an honest culture in a growing company. Thank you to all my dear team members for teaching me this lesson! You know who you are!

LESSON 2 - DON'T HIRE HUSTLERS

Hustlers can get around, get things done, and are often great at making sales. But the hustler mindset is also focused on short-term gains, cutting corners, and wheeling and dealing. They will not be your most honest employees.

The best sales lady I ever hired was a great hustler. She could independently bring in ten thousand dollars in sales per month. But she was also my worst employee. She was not dishonest. She just refused to follow procedures and thought it was absolutely fine to run her own shoe business during working hours, selling her shoes to our makeup clients. She was not a team player, but instead she was interested in growing her own sales and earnings rather than the sales of the company. I had to let her go since she stifled the whole organization. Other employees didn't get any room to develop, and she was not a great role model, despite making the best sales.

To scale up a business, I could not hire hustlers, but instead focused on finding people who were interested in becoming part of a team. I needed people ready to put the company and others ahead of their own personal, short-term gains. I needed employees who were transparent, willing to share information, and follow rules and procedures so the company could grow and scale. It meant I lost out on a lot of great talent—the best hustlers and fixers—but in return I created a steadier culture where people could grow.

LESSON 3 - SET AND ENFORCE YOUR OWN RULES

As mentioned in several chapters in this book, it is important to reduce the opportunities and temptations for employees and managers to participate in fraud and corruption. It is also essential to be able to enforce a clear tone of zero tolerance against fraud and corruption. However, from this aspect there is a major challenge within the Tanzanian judiciary system. An employer may have to wait for years, despite clear evidence of fraud or corruption, to get an employee convicted. During those years, the employer is, by law, required to continue paying the employee. If an employer goes ahead and fires an employee anyway, the company might risk a lawsuit from the employee in labor court which can take years to resolve as well.

If you can't take legal actions against fraudulent staff or fire staff who are dishonest, how do you enforce your clear tone of anti-corruption?

The solution presented to me by my local core team and HR consultants was to establish our own internal code of conduct and set up an internal labor court—called a disciplinary committee—led by the employees themselves. This was also a blessed practice by the Tanzanian labor law and a common practice among companies in Tanzania.

Firstly, all staff contracts were re-written in Swahili, and we wrote very detailed job descriptions and code of ethics. Side-hustling and theft were clearly mentioned as gross misconduct, clearing any fuzziness of right and wrong.

When an employee then broke any of these disciplinary rules, a disciplinary committee with employees from across the company was set up as a jury and conducted a hearing of the employee. In short, we basically implemented our own internal court of justice with employees as jurors and established our own notion of right and wrong. If the disciplinary committee found the evidence against an employee for theft were strong, the employee was advised to resign.

The disciplinary committee gave transparency to issues around integrity. No one was fired without getting the chance to defend him or herself, and the employees on the committee got to see the evidence of the misconduct, killing false rumors on why someone was fired. No employee refused to resign after being asked to do so by the disciplinary committee.

Code of conducts can become paper policies or real moral guidelines depending on how they are communicated and enforced. Ariely shows in numerous experiments—reminding people of code of conducts—the ten commandments and other ethical guidelines increase moral strength within a company.[61] The disciplinary committee became a forum where we repeatedly talked about dishonesty, and the committee worked in two ways: as a

---

61   *PwC US*, "Corruption of Psychology - Dan Ariely," posted on February 25, 2013, YouTube video, 24:11.

court of justice to discipline unacceptable behavior and as a reminder to employees about our code of conduct.

According to Ariely, the guilt people experience when they break rules—rules they were formerly committed to—is a much more efficient deterrent from dishonesty than punishment and fear. The employee who was heard by his or her colleagues and had broken the rules he or she had committed to live by could not feel anything else other than shame and guilt.[62]

LESSON 4 - HIRE SLOW, FIRE FAST

From late 2015 and onward, we learned to hire slow and fire fast, testing integrity early on with new employees. Atsoko was a popular place to work. For every job, we probably had two hundred applicants, so we could pick and choose.

New recruits were taken through a lengthy recruitment process. First, they were given a test, so we could check their aptitude. Based on test results, they were shortlisted and interviewed by several people in the company. Then they went through a two-week theoretical and practical training. At the end of the training they were given a new test, so that we could see what they had learned. The existing team in the stores gave their opinion on how well the recruits had managed the practical training. Recruits who were not team players, who did not show up on time, or who were lazy, showing even the smallest integrity issue, were quickly let go. The assessment of their integrity continued during the six-month probation period we had.

---

62   Ibid.

When setting up clear evaluation criteria, it was easier to involve the whole team in the recruitment process in order to not base our recruitment on bias. By involving the existing team in the recruitment, evaluation, and training processes, newcomers were socialized into Atsoko's culture. I also found my local team were much better than me in finding talents, as they had a better understanding of where new recruits came from and what the person had achieved to get a job at Atsoko. Many of our employees were school-leavers coming from quite difficult environments. They might struggle with the theoretical parts at first, but they would learn quickly on the job instead.

LESSON 5 - MANAGE PERFORMANCE

Performance management is another great tool to communicate with employees on what matters to a company. During the last years, Atsoko invested more and more in training and tracking of individual performance, so we could quickly pick up if someone was slacking. We promoted staff who performed well both on behavioral indicators and ability to meet company and individual targets.

We evaluated staff every week or month depending on what the challenges were. Some behavioral components we tracked were time management, team play, and personal appearance. Some performance measures included problem-solving skills, administrative skills, and product knowledge, on top of their sales targets or other productivity targets. Someone who did not meet their sales targets, for instance, but who was a very good team player and showed progress in learning the skills needed, was retained. Someone who delivered good results, but who did not work well with the others, or disrespected rules, were fired.

The way incentives are set up in company is pivotal for the company culture. A classic local example of when bad incentives create bad results are the local private bus companies in East Africa. In Kenya, they are called matatus. The matatu drivers get paid in cash per passenger, so they overfill their buses with people, speed, and drive recklessly. The matatus have caused the loss of many lives in traffic. Matutu drivers are known to pay off the traffic police to keep going. If you see a matatu, get out of the way.

Incentive systems are one of the trickiest things for companies to get right. Spend some time on it, and redesign if it's giving unethical results.

LESSON 6 - REDUCE TEMPTATIONS

Referring back to Chapter 2 and the fraud triangle, decreasing opportunities is an important factor in fraud and corruption prevention.[63] My auditors taught me the strategies below to reduce opportunities for employees, as well as for you as a manager, to engage in fraud or corruption unnoticed.

Reconciliations of assets and transactions are key to control any business. When you reconcile cash, stock, and other assets consistently, it is easy to find discrepancies

---

63   Koletar et al., *A.B.C.'s of Behavioral Forensics*, chapter 3, Kindle.

and to track them back to the source. If you have fraud in your organization, your reconciliations will detect them quickly, and fraudsters won't take the chance.

Stock-takes were my worst nightmare during the first three years. It took days to count thousands of products in dark storerooms, and the counts never matched. Then, I was introduced to rolling stock-take. Instead of doing one stock-take per month of our two thousand products across eight locations, we let our staff count two hundred random products spread out over about ten days of the month. By the end of the month, we had counted through the stock and could reconcile.

I probably haven't inspired you, but please just follow my advice and reconcile.

Segregation of duties should be implemented whenever there is a risk of conflict of interest. The same person should not be able to raise, confirm, and pay an invoice, for instance. Segregation of duties is probably one of the best tools to avoid fraud in high-risk environments. Still, it is important to be aware segregation might be circumvented with collusion between employees.

I was having dinner with a guy, who we can call Josef. He used to organize some of the coolest VIP parties in Dar es Salaam, where all the hip and famous went. I had been to some of his events. They were well-run and fun. As you entered, you paid one guy the entrance fee and then got a bracelet from another guy. It was a very basic segregation of duties, called a four-eyes principle. In short, it means a transaction should be approved by at least two people, reducing the opportunity for fraud.

I told him some of my early predicaments were all happening because of a lack of segregation of duties.

"What? Did you let the sales staff access the storage without any controls?" He looked at me amused and laughed at me in bewilderment.

I had let the same person handle sales and storage for some time, as I thought it was unnecessary to have one person just sitting in the storage in case we needed him or her for refills. And if I didn't give the sales staff access, I could run the risk and lose out on a sale just because the sales staff couldn't access storage to refill their shelves.

With time, I learned it was better to lose out on a sale than to have loose control over access to storage rooms. Opening up storage without control over the access was like opening a cookie jar expecting no one to touch it.

Reducing cash handling is getting easier and easier with technology, and I encourage it strongly. Despite the technological leap made by mobile money, cash was still king in Tanzania as I built Atsoko. In 2018 when I left, we made 80 percent of our sales in cash. This meant we had millions of Tanzanian shillings in cash needing to be counted, transported, and deposited in our bank account daily. There was no shortcut to this other than to set up a very strict routine. It worked well.

The bigger challenge was to control the cash expenses. It is hard to get formal receipts for a lot of services and products in an informal economy. Transport is an example of this. Our staff used bajajs (three-wheelers) or piki pikis (motorbikes) to move around. But these types of transport modes didn't give us any legal receipts. Worst case scenario, dishonest staff could use the lack of receipt to claim untrue expenses. I tried several ways to formalize this cost and found the following three options are good, depending on what technology that is available.

1. A fixed lump sum allowance for staff for transport, after estimating the cost of common routes they took. Then the staff could decide themselves if they wanted to go by bus to pocket some money or use the more luxurious bajaj or piki piki we paid for.

2. When Uber and similar services appeared during my last years in Tanzania, we used them when we could as they gave transparent reports on staff movements.

3. Recently, petty cash management apps, like Popopte Pay, have been developed for companies to monitor petty cash better in Kenya, and they work really well.

LESSON 7 - PROVIDE STAFF WITH A CUSHION AGAINST FINANCIAL PRESSURE

As the fraud triangle explains, a previously honest staff member can suddenly be pressured financially by some life event, which may make them turn to fraud or corruption.[64]

To counter sudden financial pressure, I intuitively set up a policy for employee loans. Employees could lend an amount equal to their notice period, and they could pay it off over three months. Since we had limited the loan amount to our notice period, we would issue these loans rapidly, without interest, and much additional risk for

---

64 Ibid.

us. If an employee needed more, they could approach me directly for a private loan. Quite a few of them did. I lent money for various hospital bills and for repairs of a car that had broken down, and quite a few times I lent money to employees who wanted to buy a piece of land for retirement. Sometimes there were loans repaid over a few months, and there were others repaid over a few years. I never had an employee who failed to pay me back a personal loan.

I wish more affordable healthcare scheme and employee loans by third party were available to us in Tanzania. But the healthcare insurance rates were exorbitant, often amounting to 30 percent of an employee's base salary. The interest rates on micro loans were predatory, even for formally employed staff, ranging from 15-25 percent. Like so many other things, we decided to do it ourselves to the extent we could financially do it.

By being aware of what your staff pressure points are, especially if you have low-wage staff, can help you implement safety nets, or cushions, for them to compensate for financial pressure, which could become a reason to steal.

LESSON 8 - ENCOURAGE TRANSPARENCY

Consider the following scenario: an employee has made some mistakes with the customs documentation, meaning a document is missing, and your shipment gets stopped. The customs official requests a bribe to release the shipment anyway.

If the employee is honest, he will tell you he has made a mistake and the shipment is now delayed. The customs official, however, is requesting a bribe to release it without the missing document.

If the employee does not want to take responsibility for his mistake, he will just say the customs official is corrupt and wants a bribe, and he will not mention the missing document.

With an honest employee, you could solve the problem ethically and directly by sorting out the documentation and pay any extra statutory fee due to the delay. You can be honest with the customs official and admit you made a mistake you want to rectify the legal way.

In the second case, you are made to believe the customs official is corrupt, and you don't know the delay is your own fault. If you are stressed and tired, you might believe that a bribe is the quickest solution. Or, if you have the energy, you might decide to escalate the bribery to the customs official's managers, only to find out you were at fault. Your employee has made the situation worse.

Knowing your employees operate in a very tricky environment, you need to support them and back them up if they had a good intent but made a mistake. In Tanzania, it is common for many employers to instead make their employees pay for mistakes. This can sometimes be a huge slap for the employee and make them afraid of being transparent. Encourage transparency by not punishing employees who come forward.

LESSON 9 - REWARD THE WHISTLEBLOWERS

In Atsoko, I had a couple of loyal employees who alerted me about potential internal fraud when I no longer had my own ears on the ground. In some cases, it was loyal customers who alerted me because they had seen something in my stores.

I never incentivized whistleblowers openly. I promoted the staff who kept me informed, but I never had a program where I openly recognized them. Perhaps I should have.

Oddly enough, I think I was still affected by having been brought up in a culture where you don't snitch and tell on your friends. Historically, whistleblowers have been seen and treated as persona non grata and often described as disloyal snitches reporting on colleagues as revenge or due to another less admirable motive.[65] Mario Pereira, the senior internal auditor from the telecom sector, mentioned the whistleblowers he met would often be disgruntled employees or disgruntled suppliers, and most of them didn't even come forward in person. I think our hesitant view towards whistleblowers is one of the blind truths we have to challenge, as advised by Margaret Heffernan, the author of the book on willful blindness.[66] We should encourage them.

Rewarding whistleblowers has been one way to try to clean up Wall Street after the financial crisis in 2008. Under the Dodd-Frank Act, anyone providing original information which could lead to a fine would receive a portion of that fine. One famous whistleblower in the wake of this is Ted Siedl, who made thirty million dollars on information he gave leading to a three-hundred-and-seventy million fine of JPMorgan Chase & Co. The future will tell if this was a good initiative or not.[67]

---

65 Ben McLannahan, "Best way to encourage whistleblowers? Reward them," *Financial Times*, March 5, 2019.

66 Heffernan, *Willful Blindness*.

67 McLannahan, 2019.

CONCLUSIONS

As a small business, we had to intuitively implement practices to counter dishonest behavior. I do believe, though, many of our lessons came from pure pragmatism and are useful also for larger companies.

Larger corporates might need a more structured approach to combating fraud and corruption. For them, ISO certifications, like the 37001 anti-bribery management system standard, may be very useful.

1. Get a core team that shows integrity. The people in your company will be your culture.

2. Don't hire hustlers; they will set the wrong type of culture.

3. Set and enforce clear rules. There are ways to do this.

4. Hire slow and fire fast. Invest in recruitment and training, and quickly fire employees with integrity issues.

5. Promote behavior you want and discourage behavior you don't want to have in your company.

6. Reduce temptations for staff through common internal control mechanisms, like segregation of duties and access to liquid assets such as cash and stock.

7. To relieve staff from financial pressure, try to build up a safety net for unexpected expenses for your employees, such as access to employee loans and healthcare insurance, if your company can afford it.

8. Reward a culture of openness and honesty about mistakes.

9. Reward and recognize whistleblowers

The next chapter will talk about how technology can help you in fraud and corruption prevention. I will tell about the food vendor in Dar es Salaam who monitored his staff from India. I will also discuss the importance of guarding the guards, or of watching the watcher.

CHAPTER 7

MIND THE PEOPLE WHO MIND THE SYSTEMS

Businesses of all sizes can make use of a new era of affordable and cloud-based IT systems, such as CCTV and accounting systems, to monitor fraud and corruption. But, in line with what we have learned in previous chapters, the people who design and watch these systems need to be checked. And these watchers' watchers also need to be checked, and perhaps placed somewhere far away.

LESSON 1 - CCTV USED IN A NEW WAY

I asked Mario Pereira, the internal auditor, about the most important technologies for combatting fraud and corruption. "CCTV," he said. "CCTV is one of the best things that has happened to fraud monitoring. I can monitor you in Nairobi from India for instance. The fact that people know they can be monitored also make them more careful."

A fellow entrepreneur in Tanzania—we can call him Mark—had taken CCTV to heart.

Mark was an interesting guy, to say the least. His food kiosks kept popping up next to my beauty stores, so I wanted to meet the founder of this startup.

We met over a coffee in one of the smaller malls of Dar es Salaam.

He was late and came charged with energy and distracted in the way startup entrepreneurs often are. His eyes were constantly diverting to check his phone, which kept pinging from WhatsApp messages.

"I made my money playing online poker," he said with a thick American drawl. Mark was Tanzanian but had grown up in the US.

"Really?" I asked and laughed. That wasn't at all what I had expected to hear. I leaned forward to try to figure this guy out.

"I moved to Tanzania as my dad is Tanzanian and has a hotel here. I spent the first months gambling down at the casino, but then I got bored," he explained.

Mark decided to set up a food business, both manufacturing and selling directly to clients.

He wanted to raise money to expand regionally and wondered how I had gotten investors onboard.

I started asking some questions about his business to try and understand how well run it was and became more and more impressed.

He had solved the problem of fraud, which was a big risk for his type of business, by setting up CCTV cameras monitoring his kiosks. Then, he had hired a guy in India to watch the films overnight and report the number of transactions and expected sales the next morning. This was then reconciled with what the sales team had reported. The Indian guy also counted the number of customers passing the food kiosks and the number of customers being offered to taste. In this way, Mark could also measure the conversion rate and how efficient his sales staff were in their marketing efforts.

The monitoring guy was an unknown person in India who had no other links to the company which removed the risk for collusion. Smart.

"I can introduce you to a few investors," I said.

LESSON 2 - NEW AFFORDABLE ACCOUNTING SYSTEMS

For Atsoko, CCTV was only a part of our monitoring systems. We used CCTV to follow up when something looked suspicious. I became instead more obsessed with accounting and point of sales system.

The Sarbanes Oxley Act, also called SOX, was enacted in 2002 after the Enron scandal.[68] SOX has helped to make accounting systems and internal control systems much better, according to Pereira. Accounting systems are now often cloud-based and can give real time data. The systems also have tools for more internal controls, such as seeing when people log in or make changes.

During my years with Atsoko, I also saw advanced accounting systems becoming much more accessible and

---

68 *Encyclopaedia Britannica Online,* "Enron scandal."

affordable for smaller enterprises thanks to cloud-based technologies. Atsoko didn't have to set up a private VPN network with different servers and desktop computers to implement an accounting system across our shops. We just needed Wi-Fi and some tablets.

I did quite a lot of research on different point of sales and accounting systems before settling for the system we finally implemented.

- Inventory and cash were our key fraud risks, so we needed a system to give us the real-time picture of inventory and cash to allow us to do spot checks.

- Limited access to make changes in discounts, inventory levels, pricing, and invoices issued were required.

- A system which could work offline and online was a requirement, so the sales staff could continue registering sales despite the frequent power failures in many of our shops.

I finally found a SaaS, or software as a service, which we decided to implement as our point of sales and accounting system. It was cloud based, and we could run it from laptops, tablets, and phones. Full access to the backend of the point of sales system was only given to my operations manager and myself. Other staff got access on an as-needed basis.

For larger businesses, another great and recent development is systems which can detect and assure segregation of duties, according to Pereira. For instance, if a person can both raise and approve an invoice, the systems will detect such non-segregation risks. There can also be notifications if some, for instance, approve and invoice above a certain value. For a small business like Atsoko, it was not really needed, but for larger corporate businesses it is a must.

Despite the many great systems which can combat fraud or corruption, businesses in, for instance, East Africa are not adopting it to a great extent, according to PwC survey on economic crime. A key reason is limited resources to both use the systems correctly and act on the information the systems can provide.[69]

LESSON 3 - WATCH THE WATCHER

The success of an IT system to prevent fraud and corruption comes down to one simple thing: "If you have people who can and want to circumvent the systems, and no one who watches the watcher, no IT system can save you from fraud and corruption. Mind the people who mind the systems," Bahrami, the forensic auditor, explained.

Bahrami, who worked on the forensic audit team for the money laundering investigation at Swedbank, also worked on the investigation of a large fraud scheme at Imperial Bank in Kenya. I took the chance to also get his comments on this infamous case.

Over more than a decade, 34 billion Kenyan shillings ($340 million USD) was stolen from the bank. The scandal erupted when the founder, Abdulmalek Janmohamed, died from a heart attack in his office in 2015. Janmohamed

---

69 *Fighting fraud: A never-ending battle*, PricewaterhouseCoopers, 2020.

had founded and then managed the Imperial Bank for twenty-three years. When he died, some people around him finally started talking about what had been going on in the bank, and the regulator, the Central Bank of Kenya, launched an investigation.[70]

Imperial Bank, according to Bahrami, is an example of when great systems are in use but abused. Over nine months, Bahrami and his colleagues worked around the clock uncovering the case in Nairobi. Bahrami left his hotel at 8:15 a.m. and went back at 8:30 p.m., driven in armed vehicles back and forth to Imperial Bank's head office. Considering the type of people implicated in the scam, the Central Bank was concerned about their security.

"The Imperial Bank office was a surreal place to be," said Bahrami. "The bank was formally closed, but the regulator continued to pay everyone's salary as long as they showed up for work. Thus, the employees dutifully showed up every morning, even at the branches that were closed. But since there was no work, most of them just sat at their desks watching YouTube to get paid."

Bahrami's job was to trace and visualize the money flows. In the case of the Imperial Bank, the flows were not difficult to map out. Most of the transactions had been done manually, and the execution was crude. "They had not hidden their tracks very well. First, they moved money around in the bank between different accounts, in an effort to hide the origin of funds, and finally they moved the money out. Anyone who would have looked into this would have seen it," Bahrami said. "Usually, the more

70 Paul Wafula, "How Fishmonger Family Looted Sh 34 billion from Imperial Bank" *Standard Media* December 23, 2016.

money being moved, the harder it is to trace. More middlemen are involved, and the money is moved thru more countries and jurisdictions to obfuscate the origins. But that costs money. In the case of the Imperial Bank, the main suspects were only a handful of domestic companies," Bahrami explained.

The investigators also found other, more analogous evidence, such as handwritten notes from Mr. Janmohamed to his team with instructions to do the fraudulent transfers. The notes could say: "For this week, disburse Sh100 million. Re Tilley" Nothing more was needed for the bank credit team to wire one million dollars to the Tilley account.[71]

"The truth of the matter is, you can have the best systems in the world, but if the people who are in charge of them are poorly trained or simply corrupt, it doesn't matter," Bahrami concluded. The internal staff who were supposed to monitor the system at Imperial Bank were neither incentivized nor senior enough to dare to question transactions in the way they should have.

After the scandal at the Imperial Bank erupted, shareholders questioned the officials at the Kenyan Central bank, who were supposed to supervise Imperial Bank. Several officials at the Kenyan Central Bank had, as reported in local media, soft loans and school fees paid through the Imperial Bank.[72] If true, perhaps the Kenyan Central Bank could have learned something from

---

71   Ibid.
72   "CBK fingered in Imperial Bank fraud, court reports show," *The East African*, December 23, 2016.

the food vendor, Mark. If you employ watchers to watch the banking industry and corruption is a risk, put the watchers far away so the banks can't collude with them.

LESSON 4 - TECHNOLOGY FIRST

My final lesson is to choose technology first, and then design your business processes, especially if you are a more traditional non-tech business. When we picked a SaaS for Atsoko's retail operations, we adapted our processes and organization to fit the system, not the other way around. If I would start a company from scratch today, I would look first at what software services are available and then use my system of choice as the backbone structure of my company, building the organization around the available technology. The people who designed the SaaS systems knew much more about accounting and internal controls than I did.

A mature company is harder to digitalize, but I strongly believe in digitalization, especially in environments where petty fraud is common. I recently did a due diligence of a retail company in sub-Saharan Africa for an investor. The retail operation had independent IT servers across over twenty stores, and management had no real-time information on sales, cash, or stock. They had more than forty administration staff members just shuffling papers. It was easy to see the savings that could be done with a SaaS system, both in terms of organizational efficiency and fraud prevention.

Digitalization solves many problems, like monitoring, segregation of duties, and access—all required activities to curb the opportunities for fraud and corruption, both in the private and in the public sector.

CONCLUSIONS

Tech can be very helpful for curbing fraud and corruption. In short, my recommendations are:

1. Relatively basic technology for monitoring, like CCTV, can lead to tremendous savings and change.

2. New, affordable cloud-based accounting and internal control systems should be a must for all businesses.

3. Technology also makes us more vulnerable as only a few people can create a lot of technological damage; therefore, it is important to remember to mind the people who mind the systems.

4. If you are looking at changing your business system or if you are building a new business from scratch, first have a look at the systems for accounting and internal controls available first, and then design your internal business processes.

* * *

To wrap up, I asked **Bahrami** how he sees the future of financial crime, considering the advancement in technology and new regulations.

"I'd like to think financial crime would become harder to commit. From a money laundering perspective, a cash-free society makes it much harder to launder money the way it has been done before because there is a clearer record of money flows. But, at the same time, criminals have always been at the frontier and adapted quickly to new technology, so who knows? They will probably keep adapting," Bahrami answered.

"I recently concluded a regulatory investigation into money laundering using fintech companies like Trans-ferWise and Revolut," he continued. "These companies have grown so fast their compliance efforts are having a hard time keeping up. Organized crime groups have been quick to see the opportunities and started laundering smaller but more frequent sums of money through these companies. We found one scheme where a Telco opera-tor was linked to a new fintech startup. It meant people could top up money on their phone and then transfer money from their phone to a bank account. The airtime top-up could be done from little kiosks and stores with-out much control, and lots of cash could be laundered in this way through thousands of small transactions," Bahrami gave as an example.

With this conclusion—technology is an aid, if used well, but not a cure. We will move on to the next chapter, which will address how to deal with corrupt third parties. I will give some tips and tricks on how not to be fooled by bogus suppliers, customers, and business partners.

CHAPTER 8

THINK LIKE A FRAUDSTER TO CATCH A FRAUDSTER

———

A PwC report on economic crimes from 2020 shows more than 50 percent of economic crimes experienced in the last two years by Kenyan organizations were attributed to third parties or a collusion between third parties and internal staff. The economic crimes ranged from bribery and corruption to procurement fraud and customer fraud. PwC recognized in their report this poses huge challenges for business models dependent on, for instance, outsourcing. Businesses need to consider these risks when they design their business processes and organizations.[73]

How do you control your suppliers and subcontractors? Who will you do business with? Who should you stay away from?

---

73 *Fighting fraud: A never-ending battle*, PricewaterhouseCoopers, 2020.

LESSON 1 - INTEGRATE VERTICALLY, IF YOU HAVE TO

"The check is ready," the CEO of the retail chain told me. I had harassed him with e-mails and phone calls for weeks. The retail chain was our largest reseller, with seven branches across Dar es Salaam. Their annual account with us was about one hundred thousand US dollars, so it was quite a sizeable business for us and had been working quite well for some years. But since their CFO had left, we had not been paid. Their payments were now an average of one hundred and twenty days overdue. Various excuses and explanations came each time I pushed for a payment.

Now the check was finally ready, and I let out a sigh. I sent my driver Rashid to pick it up. Their office was located close to the airport, which meant a one- to three-hour drive each way, depending on traffic. It took Rashid at least half a day to go back and forth.

He came back without a check looking tired.

"They said it wasn't signed," he said.

I lost it. It wasn't so much the money. It was the complete lack of honor of our agreement. I sent the CEO an angry e-mail. The CEO got offended and stopped buying from us from that day. That was the last client I ever offered credit to. We finally got the money though.

Retailers are notoriously bad payers in the East Africa region. For the last two decades, a couple of fast-growing Kenyan supermarkets in East Africa have used credit from suppliers to finance expansion, private-label production, and other activities. At first, the suppliers grew with the retailers, but little by little, the retailers paid less and less back to their suppliers. Since two major Kenyan-owned supermarkets, Uchumi and Nakumatt, went bankrupt with million-dollar debts to their suppliers and landlords across the region, the Kenyan regulator has recently tried to intervene. The Competition Agency has started tracking Kenyan supermarkets payment records and set the maximum credit to ninety days. The question remains how effective the regulator will be at enforcing it.[74]

My initial business plan was a distribution business. During Atsoko's first two years in business, 80 percent of our revenue came from distribution of beauty products to local retailers. However, after having spent months and months collecting overdue payments, I integrated vertically. I started expanding through more and more stores. We took the product from the manufacturer to the end customer. It was hard work, but it worked much better, and we were no longer dependent on local retailers. It strengthened our brand, and our clients benefited as well from better prices and our assurance of genuine products.

Many companies in sub-Saharan Africa have used vertical integration as a strategy and became conglomerates because of it. Ned Tozun, the co-founder and CEO of D.light, a successful solar equipment manufacturer firm, spoke at a recent seminar in Nairobi of how D.light had gone from manufacturer to distributor to a

74 Morris Kiruga, "Kenya's Tuskys on government watchlist after failing to pay suppliers," *The Africa Report,* June 19, 2020.

consumer-financing company and, most recently, a waste management company, recycling their own lamps. If you can't find the right business partners, then do it yourself.

LESSON 2 - HOLD ON TO YOUR MONEY

Another example of how distrust makes a market inefficient is the system of rent deposits in East Africa. Atsoko was renting its shop locations from large malls as well as from small private landlords. In most cases, we had to pay a deposit of two to three months' rent for each location, plus three months' rent paid in advance. When it was time to move from a location, we had to make sure to stop paying the rent up to six months prior, or whenever the payment contract we were locked in said, to get our money back. This was based on experience. The few times we failed to stop paying rent in time, we didn't get any prepaid rent or deposits back. The landlord safeguarded on his end, and we safeguarded on our end. The result was tied up working capital.

As access to finance is often expensive and constrained in high-risk markets, everyone holds on to the money they can. Interest rates in Tanzania for company loans vary from 13–25 percent, if you can even get a loan.

With time, Atsoko also started extending our payment terms to our suppliers. If we were short of cash, we paid off the smaller suppliers or the most important suppliers first. The suppliers that were large and could take a delay had to wait.

In general, I learned to manage our cash flow very carefully and cynically. All entrepreneurs need to do that, but in a market where cash is so hard to access, it becomes even more important to only let go of your cash when you really have to.

LESSON 3 - UNDERSTAND HOW COLLUSION WORKS

In some industries in some countries, collusion between employees, customers, suppliers, and government institutions is everyday business. Collusion like this is really hard to get at. A friend, we can call him Rajal, whose family has been running insurance businesses in Kenya for two generations, has experienced a fair portion of collusion between staff, clients, suppliers, and government.

In an interview, he described different schemes he has faced. "One day I drove out from an office and got hit by another driver. I called our insurance company to send an assessor to check the damages. The assessor, who didn't know who I was, called me on his way and told me, 'If you pay me 10,000 Ksh [$100], I write whatever report is needed.'" Rajal explained the scheme. "The insurance assessor colludes with the garage. The garage changes parts that don't really need replacing and hold on to the old parts. The assessor takes a cut on the extra spare parts, and the client gets an upgrade of their car. Everyone is happy, and the insurance company pays for the party. You need to be two steps ahead," Rajal said.

To counter this type of insurance fraud, Rajal's company now requests its clients to take time-stamped pictures of the incident. And they frequently rotate assessors to avoid them starting to collude with garages.

Often collusion schemes involve government institutions. Joyce, my tax advisor friend from the fourth chapter, described a collusion scheme at one company she recently audited. Once again, a case of fraud was committed within a family business.

"An employee, actually the daughter in this family business, was responsible for handling the permits for the company's trucks crossing the borders to neighboring countries Uganda and Kenya. The company was fairly large, so it was a good amount of trucks and permits processed every week," Joyce explained.

The daughter had been operating a scheme where she was inflating the actual cost for the permits in two steps: first by getting an inflated invoice for the permit through an agent at the border, and second by inflating the exchange rate for paying the permit. The permit agent, the currency broker, and the daughter then split the money.

Joyce suspects the daughter inherited the scheme when she took over the department from some other relative.

"This is a family business with very weak controls, so this could have been going on for a long time," Joyce deduced.

When Joyce and her team suspected something was off, they started comparing the costs stated for the permits with the cost of buying the same permits in bulk in Nairobi. Over six months, the daughter had made one hundred and fifty thousand dollars. "The daughter was finally caught as she transferred a lot of money to her bank account; that is how we got some evidence and could confront her," she said.

As the above and previous fraud scheme examples in this book have shown, collusions are tricky because they involve people who know the systems and can circumvent the systems better than anyone else. Many antifraud measures, like segregation of duties and monitoring, also don't work if staff, suppliers, and clients override the systems. The best ways to unveil collusion are:

1. Think like a fraudster to catch a fraudster. Where are the weaknesses in your business?

2. Have internal audits done by third parties that can't be easily corrupted.

3. Hire mystery clients that can check on a suspected scheme done by, for instance, sales staff.

4. Hire mystery suppliers that can check on your procurement staff.

5. Encourage whistleblowers inside and outside the organization.

LESSON 4 - AVOID FRAUDULENT BUSINESS PARTNERS

John is a sweet man in his late fifties. He is curious about other people, loves gossip, and is always caring. He is also an experienced accountant and former CFO who get's excited over balance sheets and reconciliation of accounts.

John lost fifty thousand dollars in less than a year to his friend and business partner, Daudi, and became involuntarily engaged both in corruption and tax evasion. How could that happen? I interviewed him for this book, as I was intrigued about his story.

"Now in arrears, I can see Daudi saw a possibility in me to defraud me. We went out, we went to nightclubs and restaurants, and he took care of me and helped me in any way possible," John said. He paused for a bit. "Funnily enough, it was always me paying."

John had been spending some years travelling frequently to Tanzania from his home in northern Europe while he was working for a European family business in Tanzania.

"I met Daudi through the family business I was working with, and we started hanging out quite a lot. He introduced me to his friends, we travelled together to Daudi's home village, and I got to see local bars and restaurants I would never have gone to on my own. Daudi was always available to me, and we had a fun time together," John said.

"Then Daudi started coming up with business ideas; it was anything from skincare to the leasing of motorbikes. Then, finally he came up with a simple business idea within micro finance which I liked. The business plan seemed credible to me, and it was a business we could scale up but still start off with a small amount of money. So, I agreed to invest, and he would start it up and run it."

John invested some money in the business. He also asked a few friends to invest with him.

The first incident occurred upon registration of the business.

"I was pushing Daudi to get the proper certifications and permits," John said. I knew it was important to get it right from the start. "But it was being delayed and delayed, then one day he just called me and said he had fixed it," John said. "I understood he must have paid a bribe, but I didn't ask."

Then after a few months, John was told about the first fraud incident in the company. The two ladies Daudi had hired to manage the lending had been skimming the clients for extra fees. Instead of Tsh 5,000 ($2), the ladies had charged Tsh 40,000 ($15) as an admin fee and pocketed the difference. The ladies were fired.

The business was slow to take off, and the setback with the sales ladies didn't help. Daudi kept asking for more money to be injected in the company. There was always a sense of urgency when Daudi requested the money, so John normally sent the money without further request.

John started asking Daudi for the accounts of the company early on, but Daudi was evasive.

"Every month I kept asking, but I never got any numbers from Daudi," John said.

The end of the first financial year was approaching, and John was now getting quite worried, as he knew the amount of compliance the business was subject to in Tanzania. Daudi kept avoiding the subject. Still, John trusted Daudi, as he thought he knew him.

John kept wiring money to keep the business afloat. Eventually John and his friends had wired all of the fifty thousand dollars they had set aside for the business but had still not gotten any proper financial records from Daudi. John confronted Daudi. By then, John had started to collect and analyze information he could access and understood there was no cash left in the business.

"I sat down at our small office with Daudi and the auditor," John said.

"This is a bit embarrassing, but where is the money?" Daudi didn't answer John, nor did the auditor John had hired to audit their accounts. John then just looked at them and asked them to leave.

"That was it for me. After that I decided to just close everything down. Daudi disappeared, and I haven't seen him since," John said, with a sad voice.

It took John almost two years to close down the business, and he had to pay several fines and fees due to the legal mess that Daudi had left behind. John is still paying back his friends, as he feels responsible for their loss.

"It was a quick way to lose fifty thousand dollars, and it was money that I didn't really have," John said, "that money was for my retirement."

Daudi is an example of a bogus business partner and rent-seeker. Daudi was a con man and used many tricks of a con man. He exploited John's wish to belong and make new friends to lure him into his business. In this book, I have discussed willful ignorance, and John's story is yet another example of that. John finally had to face the truth and Daudi's lies once all his money was gone. It was hurtful but necessary.

The only way to try to avoid bogus business partners is to do your due diligence and ask for a third-party opinion on the person. If you have the funds, hire a security firm to do a background check. Establish measures of control if you still decide to go ahead.

When you do get tangled up with a fraudster and only realize your mistake when it is too late, hire a good law firm to remove the person from your business if you still want to continue running the business. Otherwise, cut your losses and leave yourself.

LESSON 5 - AVOID BOGUS LAWYERS, AGENTS, AND FIXERS

Businesses are dependent on professional service providers, and even more so in high-risk markets. International professional services firms, like PwC, Deloitte, and KPMG, are present all over sub-Saharan Africa. My problem was they were not really catering to smaller businesses. I approached one of the firms for an annual audit and was quoted twenty-five thousand dollars. Our turnover then was just two hundred and fifty thousand dollars. Similarly, international law firms are widely available. The problem is they operate at the same rate as in Europe or the US, charging two hundred dollars per hour at least. So, for a small business, the smaller and local professional service providers are often the only option.

But then, you find yourself exposed to bogus lawyers, clearing agents, and even accountants. In an e-mail to a fellow business manager in Tanzania asking for advice about a good clearing agent, I wrote the following: *"As you probably know...not all shipping/freight agents have a clearing license...but they will tell you that they have one and then they outsource the clearing services, which often creates a mess. So do the DD."*

The best way to do the due diligence (DD) on service providers was to ask for references from like-minded companies. I was the member of the EU Business Group and also some local business networks I used for references. When hiring a consultant or an agent, I went through a process similar to a recruitment process. I asked for certificates and education, I tried to check their background on LinkedIn by checking their contacts, and then I tried them out step by step. We started with small assignments and then gave them bigger jobs, similar to a probation period with an employee. If a consultant gave advice on what we should do in a specific legal or regulatory matter, I often asked for the regulatory proof of this. If they couldn't provide this, then I could often assume they were just guessing.

CONCLUSIONS

There are so many different ways for you as a manager and as a business to be screwed over by less scrupulous players in a high-risk market. Whether you are a big or a small business, you can't afford to be the patsy. Think like a fraudster to catch the fraudster.

My core lesson is: don't be naive. It is your duty as a manager to be on the floor and to be paranoid—completely in control of who you do business with. You need to show the importance of dealing honestly with suppliers by being present and not distancing yourself from your business and your team.

In short, my tips and lessons from this chapter are:

1. Be in control of your suppliers and integrate vertically if you can't find honest business partners. Don't outsource, especially sensitive activities or business-critical activities if you can't control your suppliers

2. Hold on to your money because everyone else will.

3. Collusion between employees and third parties and between employees is very common. Make sure you rotate and verify segregation of duties. Use various internal audits and investigations to check for potential collusion. Perhaps attend some meetings between employees and suppliers every now and then, just to check on their relationship.

4. Do your due diligence on business partners who can otherwise put you in a lot of trouble. You can't assume they are honest just because they appear to be so.

5. Do your due diligence on professional service providers.

In the next and final chapter, I will dive into the unpleasantries of extortion. I will tell what connects the mafia to lemons and how I got one of my staff out of jail.

CHAPTER 9

HOW TO SAY NO TO A RACKETEER

———

Sometimes a company might feel it doesn't have a choice. They have to pay a bribe under duress. This is called extortion.

Extortion is so common in some high-risk markets I have decided to give this corrupt practice its own chapter.

When extortion becomes a way an organization conducts its business, it is called extortion racketeering—a very effective way to get money from companies or individuals. It exists all over the world—in Europe, in Africa, and in the US—and it is often led by crime organizations such as the mafia, who, with their effective methods, infiltrate entire societies or parts of societies.[75]

75 "Extortion Racketeering, E4J University Module Series: Organized Crime, Module 4: Infiltration of Organized Crime in Business and Government," UNODC, published April 2018, accessed October 9, 2020.

LESSON 1 - HOW EXTORTION RACKETEERING WORKS

How does extortion racketeering work and how does it start? To describe that, let's go back to Sicily in the 1850s.

In the 1850s, the island of Sicily had just been unified with the rest of Italy and the Italian state had not yet been able to take control of the island. Poverty was widespread and increasing civil unrest was directed toward the feudal landowners who had ruled the island for generations. At the time, Sicily had one specific industry which boomed and was ripe with money: the lemon industry. The wealthy lemon farmers became a rewarding target for attacks by the private militia. This is where the mafia's racketeering practices began.[76]

One of the first reports to the police about the emerging protection business came from a Sicilian lemon farmer in the 1850s. He had fired his warden for theft. He had then hired a new warden who was honest, but who was shot to death. He then hired a third warden who was also shot but thankfully survived. After that, the lemon farmer could not find any new warden. The lemon farmer got little help from the judiciary system. After some time, he fled from his lemon business and from Sicily.[77]

As the farmers did not get any help from a weak police force, they hired private wardens or guards to protect

76 Arcangelo Dimico et al., "Origins of the Sicilian Mafia: The Market for Lemons," *The Journal of Economic History*, Volume 77, Issue 4, (December 2017): 1083-1115.

77 *Planet Money*, "A mafia story with a twist," Podcast, posted on NPR, January 25, 2018.

their farms. These lemon wardens were recruited from the same private militia who were attacking the farmers. If the wardens paid bribes to their old friends in the private militia, the wardens and their farmers were spared from attacks. The wardens who were not loyal with the militia were shot.[78]

Initially the mafia was seen as a good movement which distributed wealth and could, thanks to this, recruit normal citizens like bankers, doctors, and lawyers. The former private militia joined the police force. As the Sicilian society was rebuilt, the mafia was suddenly everywhere and in every institution.[79]

* * *

Some corrupt government officials in Tanzania used mafia methods to extort bribes. They used their position and influence for making threats. Their extortion activities were systematic; therefore, I would call it extortion racketeering.

Amina was an eighteen-year-old Somali girl who had just finished high school when she approached me for a job as an intern in one of our stores. Her English was perfect, and she was chatty. She didn't really have any qualifications and didn't know much about makeup, but she was so persistent in requesting an internship with Atsoko that I couldn't resist her pleas.

"We need some help in the storage, if you are okay with working there," I said. "But it is a dark room without windows."

---

78 Ibid
79 Arcangelo et al.

"Yes, please!" she said enthusiastically.

Amina and her family were Somali refugees but had settled well in Dar es Salaam, and Amina had studied at a well-reputed high school.

Amina quickly learned makeup application by watching YouTube in the dark storage room during her idle time. Within a couple of months, she emerged from the storage room as a trendy young woman with a great sense of style, wearing fashionable hijabs and great makeup.

Then one day, some months after Amina had started, immigration suddenly came for a visit. They questioned why Amina didn't speak Swahili. "She can't be Tanzanian," they said.

Amina was eighteen years old when we took her in as an intern, still under her parent's passport. She was, according to the immigration officers, not legally allowed to work under her parent's documentation.

Amina's case was a typical situation of extortion. The regulations were a bit unclear, and the public officials used the fuzziness to their advantage.

Without giving us any time to clarify the situation, the immigration officers took Amina with them in their car. One of our employees followed them to see where they took her, as they wouldn't even tell us that. I tracked down Amina's parents who then went to see their daughter and the officers. The officers refused to let Amina go and even threatened to deport her, keeping Amina overnight. In the morning, an agreement was made with the immigration officers, and then Amina was released.

I'm pretty sure that if we, or Amina's parents, would have had access to an immigration lawyer who could have argued for us, Amina would not have been taken away. Extortion situations are situations of power balance. If the officers would have seen we were supported by a prestigious law firm, they might have hesitated, but at the time, we didn't have anyone to call for help.

Amina worked as a full-time employee with us after getting her own passport and then became one of our most-appreciated sales attendants.

Immigration officers came back regularly to our offices. The officers must have had informants within Atsoko or among our customers. They would come whenever we had some foreigners visiting, or when a new expat started working with us. But we had learned from what happened to Amina and avoided another ambush.

It is important to point out extortion cannot be used to excuse bribery if there hasn't been a real physical threat, according to the FCPA. If the company has the option to say no, it will not be excused; only "payments made in response to imminent threats to health or safety" are excused under the FCPA. Economic coercion or more vague threats are not considered as enough duress to excuse a bribe.[80] I'm clarifying this because companies often used extortion solicitations as an excuse to pay bribes. But, they shouldn't.

---

80 *A Resource Guide to the US Foreign Corrupt Practices Act*, page 27.

LESSON 2 - HOW TO AVOID THE AMBUSH

First, the motivations of an employee or a manager to pay or request a bribe can be several. Motivations can be personal gain or lack of discipline, but they can also be the opposite: an honest wish to achieve and do what the employee thinks is best for the company or the organization.

A study from 2018 on why public officials and business employees engage in corruption showed "the motivations for engaging in corrupt practices are surprisingly similar for the public official and the corporate employee. The most indicative factors of whether or not individuals are corruption-prone are as follows: the moral conviction they have to refrain from corruption, perceptions of whether their colleagues approve of and engage in corruption, and difficulties experienced in complying with the rules on corruption."[81]

An honest public official may ask for a bribe just because it is the easiest way for him to get his work done. I will explain. In a red-tape bureaucracy, government-issued permits often require tons of documents and several sign offs. The smallest mistake can make one of the public officials refuse to sign off an application submitted by his subordinate. An ambitious, well-meaning lower government official may advise a company to pay a small facilitation fee so he or she can make sure the internal approvals won't become a problem.

---

81 Denkers et al., "Both Sides of the Coin: Motives for Corruption Among Public Officials and Business Employees" *Journal of Business Ethics* 151, (June 14, 2016): 170-194.

During my years with Atsoko, I worked with several lower-level government officials keen on doing their job well and honestly but who worked in an organization which made it very hard for them to do so. With that in mind, to make these honest government officials' work easier, Atsoko should, in my opinion, do whatever we could to be compliant. This would also save us from the more unscrupulous government officials who would use our mistakes for extortion.

I set up a compliance department in my startup to manage the red tape and avoid ambushes. These are the steps I took:

1. I hired a person to work only with compliance and permits. In the beginning, I made the person focus on the most acute activities, like customs.

2. I established contact with lawyers in different areas of expertise to have someone to call if we got into an ambush.

3. Together with the lawyers, I discussed our regulatory compliance in detail. What were the key regulations? Who were the key government agencies and other stakeholders we had to deal with?

4. Together with my compliance manager, I mapped out the different permits each government agency required for our business activities and the estimated time and cost it would require to be compliant with permit so I could set deadlines for each permit. This compliance calendar changed frequently as regulations changed or when we expanded our business.

The agencies we needed to keep track of and liaise with where the ones with the biggest sanctions for us. These were:

1. The Tanzania Revenue Authority (TRA) had the most difficult compliance requirements. Among other things, TRA required us to file seven different taxes each month, on top of the import tax files we filed with each shipment, the daily VAT reports from our shops, and WHT on every service transaction we had, meaning there were daily, monthly, biannual, and annual compliance requirements. TRA had very long arms, wielding the power to freeze our bank accounts, to not issue our tax clearance certificate (which would stop us from trading), and to stop a shipment in customs for months.

2. The department for immigration handled my investor permit, which needed to be renewed every two years, at a cost of about five thousand dollars. The process normally took six months of preparations and follow-ups. Without this permit, I would lose the control of my business.

3. The department of labor, or more precisely the labor law, was tricky to be compliant with. As an employer, we had a range of responsibilities, and it was hard to fire anyone without due process—as I mentioned in the sixth chapter—to build an honest team, and to incentivize and discipline our staff in the right way. We needed to make sure we were compliant with the labor law.

4. In addition, there were six to seven other national agencies which had tedious processes and a number

of different permits and fees for compliance, but which couldn't directly threaten our existence. Among these, the Tanzania Food and Drug Authority (TFDA) was our biggest headache. The agency required an import registration of each individual cosmetic product we imported and sold, a permit for each consignment we imported, and a permit for each shop location. We dealt with TFDA every week when we had a consignment coming and every time we needed to register a new product.

For some of the trickiest and most risky areas, I hired lawyers and advisors on a retainer—like labor, immigration, and tax compliance—so we could call them whenever we needed. When we had a problem with a delay of a permit or something similar, I swiftly discussed with my legal advisors which escalation path we could take and what documents we needed to prepare. To me, they became an insurance plan.

Finally, I started to participate in various business networks and private sector meetings with government officials. It gave me a platform to communicate Atsoko's stance on compliance with more credibility. The lobbying effects had zero impact on regulations, but Atsoko did gain more credibility among government agencies.

Our organized and well-planned work with compliance finally gave me more time and energy to focus on the business, rather than firefighting compliance issues.

As Franz Kafka writes in *The Trial* about his bureaucratic hell, "You do not need to accept everything as true, you only have to accept it as necessary."[82] Once you accept

---

82 Franz Kafka, *The Trial*, (New York: Schocken, 2012). Kindle

compliance will cost you a significant amount of money, you might lose out on some opportunities, and compliance may have nothing to do with what is truly right, but it will make your life easier. Don't resist. Just comply.

LESSON 3 - DO YOUR RECCE BEFORE YOU ARE TOO INVESTED

There are two main things required to avoid situations of extortion when building a business: first, do your regulatory risk assessment before you invest too much money in a market, and second, if you do decide to enter a high-risk market, make sure you comply with all regulations from the start.

I recently helped an investor review a business case for a potential investment in the consumer goods industry in Nigeria. Part of my due diligence work was to check the regulatory environment. The World Bank ranks Nigeria 130th out of 190 countries in their Ease of Doing Business report.[83] This makes them slightly better than Tanzania. These World Bank reports can give some indications on the regulatory environment. To understand the actual situation for a specific sector, my belief is, however, you need to go on the field. In Nigeria, I interviewed manufacturers, suppliers, retailers, and distributors. I visited the formal market and the informal market.

All market players fingered in this case the Nigerian Food and Drug Authority (NAFDAC) as the key barrier for growth of their consumer goods sector. According to the website of the NAFDAC, the application process for

---

83 *Doing Business 2020,* The World Bank.

import should take only one to three months.[84] In reality, the market players said it could take up to two years to get all the documentation and supporting permits put together to even submit the application. The cost was also two thousand dollars in application fees, per product.

There are true barriers for entering markets like those in Nigeria and Tanzania which may scare formal players away. My interviews with various companies in Nigeria showed me despite a market with nearly two hundred million people, major consumer goods brands only distributed a small and select range of products in the market. Their explanation was of how very difficult it was to find compliant distributors. In addition, the cost and time for registration with NAFDAC just didn't make sense to them.

Similarly, because of regulatory challenges, Atsoko lost two global makeup brands in Tanzania. For almost two years, Atsoko worked with L'Oréal to get their makeup brand Maybelline registered with the TFDA in Tanzania. After eighteen months, the applications for Maybelline's two hundred makeup products were still pending, and we finally gave up as most of the products were, by then, about to be discontinued. Five years later, Maybelline dominates the makeup market in the neighboring country, Kenya. Also, Sleek MakeUP decided to withdraw from Tanzania when the company was acquired by Boots-Walgreen. The official explanation was Tanzania was no longer a priority for them. Sleek MakeUP is still one of the major makeup brands in Kenya.

84 NAFDAC, "Import Permit Application," accessed October 12, 2020.

In comparison with Tanzania, Kenya has had a much more pragmatic approach to the development of their cosmetics industry which has allowed a more formal cosmetics industry to develop. Kenya also ranks fifty-sixth in the World Bank's Ease of Doing Business report.[85] In theory, Kenya and Tanzania both belong to the East African Community's Custom Union. In reality, they are worlds apart.

While desktop research can give you an indication of how things work, some time on the ground and conversations with players in the market is needed to assess the real cost and time needed to manage the regulatory risks and the differences between markets.

Sometimes you might even need to test the ground, set up, and invest some money to get the full picture of where the regulatory risks are. Alfonso—the cement executive I wrote about in the fifth chapter—got on the ground in Nebanu but held off with investments for two years until his company had gotten all permits in a legitimate way. Mo Ibrahim, founder and CEO of Celtel, one of sub-Saharan Africa's largest telecom operators, has made similar decisions. In one market, he even invested millions of dollars to acquire the network license but then walked away after one and half years once it became clear the government would not allow them to get certain permits without bribes.[86]

Smaller businesses can learn from these larger businesses. A regulatory risk assessment is needed, whether

85 *Doing Business 2020*, the World Bank.

86 John Mullins, "Managing Ethically in Corrupt Environments." *Think at London Business School*, accessed October 9, 2020.

you are a small or a large business. Do the footwork your-self if need be before you get too invested.

If I would have done a proper regulatory due diligence before starting Atsoko in Tanzania, would I then still have set up my business there? Probably not, or maybe yes. As an entrepreneur, I have two mindsets about this. If you analyze and think too much, then you won't get anything done. At the same time, you shouldn't walk into a new market completely blind. Today, I would do a reg-ulatory due diligence, like the one I did in Nigeria, before entering any high-risk market and look at the real costs of doing business.

CONCLUSIONS

It may seem impossible at first to say no to a bribe extorted under duress, especially if you are unprepared and unsure about what the law says. But it is possible.

In this chapter I explained three ways to avoid ending up in situations of extortion and to get out of an ambush:

1. Understand the government racketeer will use your weaknesses and ignorance to pressure you. An extortion situation is a power play. If they notice you are unsure about the law and don't have anyone to call for help, they will use it to their advantage and threaten you with impris-onment and fines—threats they may not actually be allowed to issue. By knowing the law and hav-ing access to legal experts, you will get strong enough to resist most extortion situations.

Once you are invested, make sure to be compliant in order to minimize the risk of situations of extortion. It may sound like an easy task to do, but you need to understand it will take time, effort, and resources and will cost both money and opportunities to be compliant in a red-tape bureaucratic environment.

2. There is a methodology, however, to map out regulatory risks. It is not as fuzzy and impossible as it may first seem. By reviewing the regulatory environment in detail, you will be one step ahead of the government officials. They may still apply the law unfairly, but then you can choose to appeal and make their life difficult. After some time, they will turn to other weaker victims.

3. I started this chapter with a tale about the origins of the mafia in Sicily to explain how extortion works but also to explain the importance of doing your business-risk due diligence before you invest too much in a market. It takes three to five years for a lemon tree to bear fruit. Lemon trees require a lot of care. By nature, a lemon tree is a fixed and vulnerable asset the lemon farmer cannot take with him if he suddenly finds himself in situation where he either needs to accept extortion and bribery or leave. Before you get too vulnerable and grow those trees, try to understand what the risks of threat or corruption are and what situations of extortion you may encounter so you don't end up in an ambush where you will feel you have too much too lose to say no. You might have to go on the ground to do this, but don't invest too much before you know what type of environment you are entering.

It may feel hard for a local or smaller business to be compliant and resist extortion. I know that because I have been there. A small company will not have the same resources as larger businesses to manage their compliance and make legal appeals. But by trying to be compliant and making efforts of resistance, a small business owner can at least end up in less situations of extortion and stay clear of the slippery slope of bribes and fraud following.

SUMMARY

This book has been my redemption song—my journey into trying to understand what I learned from building a company from scratch in a high-risk market. It is not my intention to discourage the private sector from investing in high-risk markets but rather the opposite. The private sector is driving development and innovation and is crucial for bringing resources, knowledge, and know-how across the world. The objective of this book is for investors, entrepreneurs, and managers to venture into high-risk markets with their eyes wide open, understanding what resources they will need to do it right.

WHY I WROTE THIS BOOK

I had to dedicate tremendous time and effort to managing petty fraud and corruption in my startup in Tanzania. It was painful. After two or three years of managing it haphazardly, I slowly started to understand it was me. I, as the founder and manager, had to strategically resource my company and my team to deal with the recurring fraud and corruption risks.

IT'S NOT ALWAYS ABOUT THE MONEY

Before my years in Tanzania, and before writing this book, I thought greed was the major motivator for people engaging in fraud and corruption, but my experiences and the research I have done for this book have given me a much more nuanced understanding. The motivation can range from money, to feeling pressure to achieve, to a search for excitement, or to a wish for belonging and love. With a better understanding of what motivates people to engage in fraud, managers who know their employees can also better detect staff who are at risk.

DON'T LIE TO YOURSELF

Rationalizations help us transform our own harmful practices into good deeds. We come up with a range of excuses to why we had to pay that bribe or why it was not so bad after all to book a holiday as a business trip. We think about ourselves as good people, but we all have an itch for the forbidden fruit. Just because we falter sometimes doesn't mean we should consider ourselves bad people; so, we tell ourselves that we are not. If rationalizations are done well, they make us blind to what we have done.

OPEN YOUR EYES

Humans are not rational. Our brains are not able to handle too many conflicting interests or emotions at once, and therefore, they decide to block out what disturbs us. We make ourselves partially blind to help ourselves cope with emotions like hurt, shame, and guilt. This mechanism is called willful blindness and is relevant to understanding fraud and corruption because it can make owners, managers, and employees ignore the crimes happening in their business.[87]

SET THE TONE

It is harder than you think to walk the talk as a manager. Implementing a credible anti-corruption policy might mean a company will lose out on business or time. If the board and management are not prepared to risk those costs and miss some opportunities, they won't be able to keep a clear tone. A manager needs support from the board and should not be incentivized to make shortcuts. Finally, a manager needs to know his or her weaknesses and desires and learn to manage them.

BUILD AN HONEST TEAM

Once you have set a clear tone, clear rules, and provided adequate resources from the top, you need to make sure you hire people who agree with your values and are ready to live and work by them. You then consciously and consistently invest in their training and reward not only based on financial targets but on how the people behaved to get there. You encourage honesty and transparency by not punishing mistakes and by rewarding whistleblowers.

MIND THE PEOPLE WHO MIND THE SYSTEMS

Software as a service (SaaS), smart CCTV, and other IT solutions for businesses have made fraud and corruption

---

87 Heffernan, *Willful Blindness.*

prevention easier. However, the systems are only as good as the people managing them. Mind the people who mind the system is a core lesson.

THINK LIKE A FRAUDSTER TO CATCH A FRAUDSTER

There are so many different ways for you to be screwed over by unscrupulous players in a high-risk market. Whether you are a big or a small business, you can't afford to be the patsy. Think like a fraudster to catch the fraudster. Don't be naïve. Do your due diligence. It is your duty as a manager to be on the floor, paranoid and in control of who you do business with. You need to show the importance of dealing honestly with third parties by being present and not distancing yourself from the business and your team.

HOW TO SAY NO TO A RACKETEER

Coercion or extortion of a bribe under duress is common in markets with a corrupt public administration. You might find yourself forced to pay bribes to get employees out of jail or wait several years for permits. Some industries and markets may even be too corrupt to crack. The more a company has already invested, the more vulnerable it is to threats of extortion if it has not done its risk mitigation. If you do decide to enter a high-risk market, try to understand what the environmental, social, and governance risks are *before* you invest too much and set up a strategy for how to deal with them. This may save you from getting into an ambush when you have too much to lose to dare to say no.

IN SHORT

You may remember Charlotte, the manager who paid a bribe and was blacklisted by the World Bank for corruption. You may also remember Alfonso, the cement plant manager who waited two years for a permit. Charlotte was pressured by time, fatigue, and a manager who didn't listen to her concerns. Alfonso was supported by executives who understood the long-term risks of bribery and didn't pressure or incentivize him to take shortcuts. His executives even flew in to assist him when he was extorted for a bribe. My key message with this book is that a manager without the right resources and tools to manage corruption and fraud will very likely fall victim to corruption and fraud in a high-risk market. A proper recce of the risks, a good strategy linked with the right resources, and enough time and patience will help a manager navigating most fraud and corruption risks in high-risk markets. Ignorance is not an excuse under the law and certainly isn't for an investment gone wrong.

EPILOGUE

How does a new president matter to a small business in Tanzania? A lot.

President Dr. John Magufuli took office in 2015 and promised to modernize and industrialize Tanzania and clean up the corrupt administration. The slogan for his election campaign was "hapa kazi tu," which means "here, it's work only," meaning hard work is needed to drive the economy and development forwards. Most people didn't think much about it at first. After all, President Magufuli was a politician from the Chama cha Mapinduzi (CCM) party—the political party who has ruled Tanzania since its independence. President Magufuli had also been a minister in his predecessor's, President Kikwete's, government. So, how different could he be?

It turned out President Magufuli would take everyone by surprise, including his own party. In his first ninety days in office, he fired corrupt officials, slashed lavish government allowances, and cancelled the celebrations of the national independence day, saying military parades were a waste of money. Instead he instituted a national cleaning day and went out himself to sweep the streets of Dar es Salaam. He continued to clean out ten thousand ghost workers in the public administration.[88,89]

---

88 "Tanzania purges 10,000 'ghost workers' in anti-corruption drive," *BBC News,* May 16, 2016.

89 "Tanzania President John Magufuli helps clean streets," *BBC News,* December 9, 2015.

Was he for real? The Tanzanian and the international business communities stood wide-eyed and hesitantly cheered him on. Skeptics said, "Ni Nguvu ya soda," meaning his frenzied activities were just a soda fizz. This would pass.

President Magufuli was true. He was not only true to his quest against corruption in the public sector, he would also go on to root out tax evasion, corruption, and fraudulent practices in the private sector. He asserted he would improve tax revenue collection and use the money to develop Tanzania. His goals were applaudable; however, the methods he would use to reach them were not. He would hit down hard and arbitrarily on the private sector.

THE TAX APPEAL

The first sign of this new arbitrary rule of law arrived on my desk on January 18, 2016.

It was a demand note from the Tanzanian Tax Revenue Authorities (TRA) stating Atsoko should pay an amount equal to $130,000 within seven days. The amount was based on an assessment done by the TRA and consisted of a combination of taxes, fees, interests, and fines. In short, the tax authorities stated that Atsoko had evaded taxes and was therefore being heavily fined and penalized for tax evasion.

The morning after, I got up early and went to my favorite breakfast place, the Epi d'or cafe in Dar es Salaam. They had the best pain au chocolat and cappuccino in town, and I liked to start my days there in the shade, getting some work done as the day started to warm up.

I pondered over my options. I figured I first needed to understand if this demand note was legitimate or if it was just an attempt of extortion. But I had not, to my knowledge, been approached for a bribe in this case. I took my phone and called a local tax advisor I had recently been introduced to. I told him about the demand note and asked for advice.

The tax advisor sounded stressed and was not very empathetic. He told me I had to pay an objection fee equal to 30 percent of the amount if I wanted to object to the assessment.

"It can't be true," I said. "I haven't even seen the assessment they base their demand on or been given the chance to respond."

The tax advisor answered, with this new government in power, I should just cooperate with the TRA. The TRA could freeze our bank accounts if we didn't.

Could this be true? Could the tax authorities be allowed to issue arbitrary tax assessments without giving a company a chance to be heard and defend themselves? If they did, they ignored their own principles of natural justice stated in the Tanzanian law itself. Tanzanian tax law stipulated these principles very clearly. A company should first be given time to review and object to a tax assessment before it was issued, and thereafter get thirty days to respond to a final assessment before a demand note was sent out. I had never been given any draft or any final assessment to review. I had been given no chance to defend my company.

When I hung up, I started crying.

I left it for a few days and then raised my concern with the unfriendly debt collectors from the TRA who'd came back to remind us about the payment. They were prepared. They referred to a hand-written delivery note signed off by one of our shop attendants as a proof of delivery of the tax assessment. When confronted, the shop attendant said she hadn't received anything. Regardless of who was telling the truth, I found it strange that a $130,000 tax assessment could be "deemed to be delivered" when handed to a shop attendant and not directly to me, the CEO of the company.

After some time, I did get a copy of the tax assessment in my hand. Besides assuming our startup capital was revenue and including several other odd conclusions, it also contained major computing errors. I was at a loss. The whole tax affair was a truly Kafkaesque experience.

After some months of fruitless efforts to speak with the TRA officials at our tax office, I needed to ask some powerful friends to help me out.

I sought out one of the top tax lawyers in Tanzania whom I vaguely knew and couldn't really afford to hire. We met early in the morning—at 8:00 a.m.—at his fancy office in one of the skyscrapers in town. I had gotten up at 5:30 a.m. to be there on time. My eyes were gritty from the lack of sleep, and I gratefully sipped the hot and sweet masala tea that was served. I pleaded for help.

The lawyer agreed to take on my case at a fixed fee of $10,000 and said Atsoko had a good case for an appeal to the Tax Revenue Appeal Board. We had clearly not been given a fair chance to be heard, and there were some obvious weaknesses in the assessment. He also advised me to get a new auditor and accountant to review my books.

"If the TRA agrees to reopen your case, you need to have everything in order so you can present your evidence without delays," he said.

Atsoko filed in late April for an official objection to the tax claim, which was rejected by the TRA. In June 2016, we submitted an appeal to the Tax Revenue Appeals Board to reconsider our case. Atsoko's appeal to be heard before sentenced stayed at the bottom of a heap of hundreds of other similar appeals, until I sold the business in early 2018.

* * *

In 2016, I met and fell in love with Robert, a former British army officer, and in 2017, we were expecting our first child. The political development in Tanzania frightened me, and I started to doubt if I could risk making Atsoko my life's work. I could fight petty fraud and corruption, but I could not fight against a government with no respect for the principles of justice. I also noticed a dwindling interest among investors to invest in Tanzania and a new skepticism towards investing in Atsoko. My pregnancy and my own ambivalence also probably didn't help to convince investors.

I made the difficult decision to sell my shares in Atsoko and leave my team in early 2018. The future will tell if I avoided a bullet or if Tanzania will rise again. Atsoko is still there in Tanzania, run by my former team under new ownership, which makes me very happy to see. Atsoko didn't become my life's work, but hopefully the work for generations to come.

ACKNOWLEDGEMENTS

——

Thank you to my love, Robert, for providing for our little family while I locked myself up to write this book. Without you I would never have taken the time to do this. Xxxxxxxx

I'm forever grateful to all of you who believed enough in me and in this book to order it even before it was written. Your support got me through the difficult days when this book project felt too daunting and forced me to finish what I had started.

My Super Sponsors

Katarina Kahlmann

Jesper Drescher

Ted Persson

Mario Pereira

Linda Fors

My Sponsors

Ammar Adhami

Marcus Adolfsson

Samira Aissi

Philip Ajina

Sofia Alexus

Emily Almhagen

Anna Berlin

Mikael Berlin

Monica Blaalid

Elisabeth Blennow-Calälv

Ludvig Bontell

Carsten Bremer

Sofia Altafi

Björn Andersson

Florian Andriessen

Clive Ashmore

Martin Aurelius

Kerstin Axelsson

Sina Bahrami

Peter Barker

Bruno Beijer

Niklas Bergman

Sabrina Dorman

Celine Doutriaux

Emma Dufva

Mai Duong

Lauritz Elmshäuser

Peter Englesson

Maria Friström

Aleksandra Fundi

Andreas Giallourakis

Charlotte Grane

Percy Grundy

Erlend K. Haugen

Jean Francois Hellivan

Staffan Hillberg

Mathias Holmgren

Sandra Holtenfjord

Jessica Hurtig

Liz Hutchinson

John Jakobsson

Frida Jangsten

Peter Carlstedt

Anna Castberg

Cecilia Cederlid

Patricia Chin-Sweeney

Joshua Chipman

Ronald Claes

Marika Cullin

Melker Cullin

Pia Cullin

Philippe D'Have

Josefine Karlsson

Jaime Keating

Paula Kermfors

Erasto Kimambo

Mathilda Klingberg

Claire Krawsczyn

Ted Kristensson

Katrin Kuhlmann

Moa Lagercrantz

Nina C. Lande

Marie Lasku

MacGregor Lennarz

Magnus Lien

Mathias Lienard

Wilhelm Löwenhielm

Daniel Lövquist

Miriam Lund

Raj Manek

Kathleen Mckendrick

Sara Mpumwire

Zhelu Jia
David Johansson
Filip Johansson
Lina Jorheden
Steven Jurgens
Christian Karlander
Anna Ohlsson-Baskerville
Magnus Omstedt
Caroline Örberg
Lina Palmer
Esther Palsgraaf
Henie Parillon
Jussi Rasinmäki
Kush Ratna
Xavier Rocoplan
Anders Roos
Therese Sandmark
Simon Schmid
Anna Schoeffler
Emilie Westholm
Louise Yngström Valdre

Simon Mtabazi
Susan Mwangi
Charles Mwebeiha
Andreas Nabseth
Ida Nilsson
David Notman
Jenny Sjöberg
Emil Sjöblom
Martin Söderberg
Harald Stenbacka
Josephine Sundqvist
David Svaninger
Maria Svemark
Filip Tack
Arjan Tiessen
Maarten Uyttendaele
Pim Valdre
Monica Vidal
Joel Westerström
Luke Wilde

I'm equally grateful to you, my interviewees, who made this book possible and so much more relevant by sharing your insights, time, and wisdom. Sina Bahrami, Philippe Montigny, Mario Pereira, Alfonso Rodriguez, Kang'e Saiti, "Charlotte", "Joyce", "John", "Mark", "Rajal".

Lin Lerpold and Carin Sjölin from the Stockholm School of Economics: thank you so much for your time, your kind interest in my project, and for sharing the relevant academic research and literature on corruption and business ethics.

Anton Mifsud-Bonnici and Dorothy Gaulin: thank you for introducing me to your anti-corruption resources and networks. Really helpful!

A special thanks to my cheerleaders and early readers Neha Kumar, Antonia Mundawarara, and Dave Mark who read my first terrible drafts and came with their smart input.

Rania and Pelle, I'm so thankful to you for letting me use your kitchen as my writer's hideout. I especially appreciated your stock of chocolate bars.

Ram Lokan, my fellow author and entrepreneur, what a great idea to get on the Creator Institute book writer program and share this experience with me. I'm particularly grateful for your frequent WhatsApp messages at 6 a.m. that got me out of bed to start writing.

Eric Koester, you are a great book professor. You made the whole writing experience fun and so much less daunting. Then, my humble gratitude to my editors, Margaret Danko and Sarah Lobrot, who actually made we write this book. Thank you for cheerleading and nagging me; thank you for your patience and for pushing me to be better. Also, a big thank you to the whole New Degree Press publishing team for believing in my book idea, and for making my book look so professional.

Last, but not least, I send my warmest thanks to all my staff, friends, advisors, investors and everyone else who helped me build Atsoko, all of you who worked with me to build the great company that we are all so very proud of. I miss you. You know who you are! Xxxxxx

And by the way, I guess I have to thank also you—fraudsters, rent seekers, and racketeers—who inspired me to write this book. You certainly opened my eyes to the darker sides of the fascinating human mind, and also made me see my own weaknesses. Together with you I never had a boring day. I hope you know who you are.

Yours sincerely,

Marie Englesson

BIBLIOGRAPHY

Introduction

Cassin, Harry. "Airbus shatters the FCPA top ten." *The FCPA Blog*, February 3, 2020. https://fcpablog.com/2020/02/03/airbus-shatters-the-fcpa-top-ten

Montero, David. *Kickback: Exposing the Global Corporate Bribery Network*. New York: Viking, 2018. Kindle.

OECD. "OECD Convention on Combating Bribery of Foreign Public Officials in International Business Transactions." Accessed September 28, 2020. http://www.oecd.org/corruption/oecdantibriberyconvention.htm

PricewaterhouseCoopers. Fraud: The overlooked competitor, Global Economic Crime and Fraud Survey, Tanzania, 2018. Dar es Salaam: 2018. Accessed October 20, 2020. https://www.pwc.co.tz/assets/pdf/gecs-2018-report.pdf

PricewaterhouseCoopers. *Fighting fraud: A never-ending battle, Global Economic Crime and Fraud Survey, 2020.* 2020. Accessed October 20, 2020. https://www.pwc.com/gx/en/forensics/gecs-2020/pdf/global-economic-crime-and-fraud-survey-2020.pdf

Saminather, Nicola, Shabalala, Zandi. "Barrick's offer for Acacia Mining reflects Tanzania risk: CEO." *Reuters*, May 24, 2019. https://www.reuters.com/article/us-acacia-mining-barrick-gold-idUSKCN1SU1NK

Sturgis, Sam. "The Bright Future of Dar es Salaam, an Unlikely African Megacity." *Bloomberg CityLab*, February 25, 2015. https://www.bloomberg.com/news/articles/2015-02-25/tanzania-s-dar-es-salaam-is-on-track-to-become-one-of-africa-s-most-important-megacities

The World Bank. *Doing Business 2015: Going Beyond Efficiency.* Washington DC: 2014. Accessed October 20, 2020. https://www.doingbusiness.org/content/dam/doingBusiness/media/Annual-Reports/English/DB15-Full-Report.pdf

Transparency International. "Corruption Perceptions Index, Tanzania, 2015." Accessed September 21, 2020. https://www.transparency.org/en/cpi/2015/results/tza

Chapter 1

Encyclopaedia Britannica Online. Academic ed. s.v. "Fraud." Accessed October 10, 2020. https://www.britannica.com/topic/fraud

PricewaterhouseCoopers. *Fraud: The overlooked competitor, Global Economic Crime and Fraud Survey, Tanzania, 2018.* Dar es Salaam: 2018. Accessed October 20, 2020. https://www.pwc.co.tz/assets/pdf/gecs-2018-report.pdf

Transparency International. "Petty Corruption." Accessed June 15, 2020. https://www.transparency.org/en/corruptionary/petty-corruption

Transparency International. "Extortion." Accessed on October 10, 2020. https://www.transparency.org/en/corruptionary/extortion

Transparency International. "What is corruption." Accessed October 10, 2020. https://www.transparency.org/en/what-is-corruption

Transparency International. "Nepotism." Accessed on October 10, 2020. https://www.transparency.org/en/corruptionary/nepotism

US Department of Justice and US Securities and Exchange Commission. *A Resource Guide to the U.S Foreign Corrupt Practices Act.* Washington DC: 2012. https://www.sec.gov/spotlight/fcpa/fcpa-resource-guide.pdf

Chapter 2

Ariely, Dan. *The (Honest) Truth About Dishonesty: How We Lie to Everyone—Especially Ourselves.* New York: HarperCollins, 2012. Kindle

Coenen, Tracy. "How to Detect Behavioral Red Flags of Fraud." *Fraud Files Forensic Accounting Blog.* Sequence Inc. April 12, 2016. https://www.sequenceinc.com/fraudfiles/2016/04/how-to-detect-behavioral-red-flags-of-fraud/.

Koletar, Joseph W., Morrison, David E., Pope, Kelly R., Ramamoorti, Sridhar. *A.B.C.'s of Behavioral Forensics: Applying Psychology to Financial Fraud Prevention and Detection.* New York: Wiley, 2013. Kindle.

Noah, Trevor. *Born a Crime: Stories from a South African Childhood.* London: One World, 2016. Kindle.

PricewaterhouseCoopers. *Fighting fraud: A never-ending battle, Global Economic Crime and Fraud Survey, 2020.* 2020. Accessed October 20, 2020. https://www.pwc.com/gx/en/forensics/gecs-2020/pdf/global-economic-crime-and-fraud-survey-2020.pdf

The World Bank. "Poverty." Accessed October 10, 2020. https://www.worldbank.org/en/topic/poverty/overview

Chapter 3

Anand, Vikas, Ashforth, Blake E., Joshi Mahendra. "Business as usual: The acceptance and perpetuation of corruption in organizations" *Academy of Management Executive*, 18, No. 2 (2004): 39-53. https://www.lawschool.cornell.edu/alumni/reunion/upload/04anand_et_al-_ame_2004.pdf

London Real TV. "The Corruption Test – Dan Ariely." Posted on March 30, 2018. YouTube video. 4:45. https://youtu.be/2kk-mgmvSWPQ

Chapter 4

Almgren, Jan. "Utredning mot Bonnesen växer – åtal närmar sig," *Svenska Dagbladet*, August 24, 2020. https://www.svd.se/utredning-mot-bonnesen-vaxer—atal-narmar-sig

Encyclopaedia Britannica Online. Academic ed. s.v. "Elizabeth Holmes." Accessed September 21, 2020. https://www.britannica.com/biography/Elizabeth-Holmes.

Encyclopaedia Britannica Online. Peter Bondarenko. s.v. "Enron scandal." Accessed September 21, 2020. https://www.britannica.com/event/Enron-scandal.

Goncharenko, Roman. "Magnitsky a symbol of sanctions — and not just in Russia." *Deutsche Welle*, November 16, 2019. https://www.dw.com/en/magnitsky-a-symbol-of-sanctions-and-not-just-in-russia/a-51267181

Heffernan, Margaret. Willful Blindness: *Why We Ignore the Obvious at Our Peril*. London: Simon & Schuster, 2011. Kindle.

London Real TV. "The Corruption Test – Dan Ariely." Posted on March 30, 2018. YouTube video. 4:45. https://youtu.be/2kk-mgmvSWPQ

McLannahan, Ben. "Best way to encourage whistleblowers? Reward them." *Financial Times*. March 5, 2019. https://www.ft.com/content/cac4c994-3f24-11e9-9bee-efab61506f44.

Swedish Public Television (SVT). Uppdrag granskning. Season 21, episode 12. "Swedbank och penningtvätten." posted on April 15, 2020, TV-program. https://www.svtplay.se/video/26409222/uppdrag-granskning/uppdrag-granskning-sasong-21-avsnitt-12

Zimbardo, Philip. *The Lucifer Effect: How Good People Turn Evil*. London: Random House, 2009.

Chapter 5

Alderman, Liz. "Terrorism Financing Charge Upheld Against French Company Lafarge." *The New York Times*. November 7, 2019. https://www.nytimes.com/2019/11/07/business/lafarge-terrorism-syria.html

ISO. "ISO 37001 Anti-bribery-management." Accessed October 12, 2020. https://www.iso.org/iso-37001-anti-bribery-management.html

Montigny, Philippe. *Integrity for Competitiveness: on the road with compliance officers*. Paris; ETHIC Intelligence Publishing, 2018.

Venard, Bertrand. "Lessons from the massive Siemens corruption scandal one decade later." *The Conversation*. December 13, 2018. https://theconversation.com/lessons-from-the-massive-siemens-corruption-scandal-one-decade-later-108694

Chapter 6

Heffernan, Margaret. *Willful Blindness: Why We Ignore the Obvious at Our Peril*. London: Simon & Schuster, 2011. Kindle.

Koletar, Joseph W., Morrison, David E., Pope, Kelly R., Ramamoorti, Sridhar. *A.B.C.'s of Behavioral Forensics: Applying Psychology to Financial Fraud Prevention and Detection*. New York: Wiley, 2013. Kindle.

McLannahan, Ben. "Best way to encourage whistleblowers? Reward them." *Financial Times*. March 5, 2019. https://www.ft.com/content/cac4c994-3f24-11e9-9bee-efab61506f44.

PwC US. "Corruption of Psychology – Dan Ariely.". Posted February 25, 2013. YouTube video. 24:11. https://www.youtube.com/watch?v=pXsJ-6YCFSU

Chapter 7

Encyclopaedia Britannica Online. Peter Bondarenko. s.v. "Enron scandal." Accessed September 21, 2020. https://www. britannica.com/event/Enron-scandal.

PricewaterhouseCoopers. *Fighting fraud: A never-ending battle, Global Economic Crime and Fraud Survey, 2020.* 2020. Accessed October 20, 2020. https://www.pwc.com/ gx/en/forensics/gecs-2020/pdf/global-economic-crime-and-fraud-survey-2020.pdf

Wafula, Paul. "How Fishmonger Family Looted Sh 34 billion from Imperial Bank." *Standard Media*. December 23, 2016. https://www.standardmedia.co.ke/business/ article/2000187824/how-fishmonger-family-looted-sh34-billion-from-imperial-bank

The East African. "CBK fingered in Imperial Bank fraud, court reports show." December 23, 2016. https://www. theeastafrican.co.ke/tea/business/cbk-fingered-in-imperial-bank-fraud-court-reports-show—1359740

Chapter 8

PricewaterhouseCoopers. *Fighting fraud: A never-ending battle, Global Economic Crime and Fraud Survey, 2020.* 2020. Accessed October 20, 2020. https://www.pwc.com/ gx/en/forensics/gecs-2020/pdf/global-economic-crime-and-fraud-survey-2020.pdf

Morris Kiruga, "Kenya's Tuskys on government watchlist after failing to pay suppliers" *The Africa Report.* June 19, 2020. https://www.theafricareport.com/30456/kenyas-tuskys-on-government-watchlist-after-failing-to-pay-suppliers/

Chapter 9

Denkers, Adriaan, Gorsira Madelijne, Huisman Wim. "Both Sides of the Coin: Motives for Corruption Among Public

Officials and Business Employees" *Journal of Business Ethics* 151 (June 14, 2016): 170-194. https://link.springer.com/article/10.1007/s10551-016-3219-2

Dimico, Arcangelo, Isopi Alessia , Olsson Ola. "Origins of the Sicilian Mafia: The Market for Lemons." *The Journal of Economic History* 77, Issue 4 (December, 2017): 1083-1115. https://www.cambridge.org/core/services/aop-cambridge-core/content/view/52B18A611BD8AE26B4FDE3814A4239F1/S002205071700078Xa.pdf/origins_of_the_sicilian_mafia_the_market_for_lemons.pdf

Kafka, Franz. *The Trial*. New York: Schocken, 2012. Kindle

Mullins, John. "Managing Ethically in Corrupt Environments." *Think at London Business School*. Published July 3, 2012. Accessed October 9, 2020. https://www.london.edu/think/managing-ethically-in-corrupt-environments

Planet Money. "A mafia story with a twist." Podcast. Posted on NPR, January 25, 2018. https://www.npr.org/2018/01/25/580820776/a-mafia-story-with-a-twist

The World Bank. *Doing Business 2020: Comparing Business Regulation in 190 Economies*. Washington DC: 2020. https://www.doingbusiness.org/en/reports/global-reports/doing-business-2020

UNODC. "Extortion Racketeering, E4J University Module Series: Organized Crime, Module 4: Infiltration of Organized Crime in Business and Government." Published April 2018. Accessed October 9, 2020. https://www.unodc.org/e4j/en/organized-crime/module-4/key-issues/extortion-racketeering.html.

US Department of Justice and US Securities and Exchange Commission. *A Resource Guide to the U.S Foreign Corrupt Practices Act*. Washington DC, 2012) https://www.sec.gov/spotlight/fcpa/fcpa-resource-guide.pdf

Summary

Heffernan, Margaret. *Willful Blindness: Why We Ignore the Obvious at Our Peril.* London: Simon & Schuster, 2011. Kindle.

Epilogue

BBC News. "Tanzania purges 10,000 'ghost workers' in anti-corruption drive." May 16, 2016. https://www.bbc.com/news/world-africa-36303031

BBC News. "Tanzania President John Magufuli helps clean streets." December 9, 2015. //www.bbc.com/news/world-africa-35049628

Lightning Source UK Ltd.
Milton Keynes UK
UKHW020246241220
375730UK00007B/167